LIFTING THE VEIL

DAVID ICKE

Interviewed by
JON RAPPOPORT

TS **Truth Seeker**
Books SAN DIEGO, CALIFORNIA

LIFTING THE VEIL:
DAVID ICKE INTERVIEWED BY JON RAPPOPORT
Copyright © 1998 by Truth Seeker Co., Inc.

Cover design by David Sielaff

ISBN: 0-939040-05-0

Printed in the UK
Produced by Namaste Publishing – UK
P. O. Box 127, Shrewsbury SY3 7WS
Tel: 01743-341303

10 9 8 7 6 5 4 3 2 1

To Bonnie Lange,
the Truth Seeking never stops

LIFTING THE VEIL

DAVID ICKE

Interviewed by
JON RAPPOPORT

October 1997

Contents

Introduction by Jon Rappoport 2

Diana: Murdered by the Brotherhood? 7

The Brotherhood Agenda 12

The Origin of the Brotherhood 19

Stealing the Knowledge 24

Why the United States Has
    NEVER Been Free 34

Sign and Symbols of "Brotherhood"
    America 38

The Brotherhood Pyramid 43

The Robber Barons 50

The Brotherhood of Knowledge 59

The Mind Doctors 63

The Mind Controlled Assassins 77

Breaking the Spirit 81

Ritual Child Abuse 83

The Big Picture 88

New Age Naiveté 94

Two Sides of the Same Face 100

What Future Do You Want? 103

Another Brick in the Wall 107

Journey of Discovery 109

The Ridicule Years 124

The Human Herd 128

Building the Sheep Pen 130

A Time to Awaken 132

Introduction

by Jon Rappoport

There is a growing number of researchers and writers who start from the premise that the world we are given is not the true world.

After fifteen years as an investigative reporter, I have found very few people who not only form a set of ideas to explain our world, but then back them up with action.

I have seen men and women who fall into a state of decay because their hard-won truth rots on the vine. They somehow labor under the self-imposed delusion that once they have presented their vision, it is up to others to implement it. That is a danger-ous place to be, because in the end you are left with a big room and no one else in it. Then come the ugly vanity and the excuses and the resent-ments and the accusations and the mirrors of despair.

David Icke has taken the other road.

He has the energy for it. He goes out on the road and he lets loose with his findings and his ideas and his vision and his research. He connects with people. They want to hear what he has to say because they sense his growing confidence that he is on the right track.

David does not worry about the little things. He doesn't care if people disagree with him on certain points. He doesn't back off because it's Monday and the rain is coming down and the hotel is full and the car didn't arrive and the hall they hired didn't have the right sound system. He stands up there and starts talking and pretty soon the audience is mesmerized because they hear his truth coming out and they see that what he is saying fits a pattern of power that is operating behind the scenes of this world.

When I sat down and did these interviews with him, I found I didn't care that he and I didn't mesh on all points. So what? There was a more expansive energy going on, and on that level we were in agreement. We saw the same crazy world dominated by fewer and fewer people, and we saw that there was a way out of this mess that involves every one of us. We saw that the mess was social and political and psychological and anergic and spiritual and you couldn't carve it up into little pieces and play cat and mouse games with it. You couldn't divide the mess into disciplines and appoint people to chairs of professorship and rant and rave in a vacuum.

You had to connect with people and force the issue. You had to wake people up, and then you would wake yourself up. And the other way too. You had to get in there and mix it up and start talking about solutions, and you couldn't be afraid of the personal spiritual side of things and you couldn't be terrified of introducing the hard political and, yes, conspiratorial, factors into the mix. David does both. He doesn't hold back. He doesn't try to erase the bad things that are going on in favor of a saccharine tune, and he damn well doesn't claim that only matter is real and there is no spirit. He has experienced for himself both sides.

I like people like that, because they are heading down the main highway of life. they are not democrats or republicans, they are not right or left, they are not New Age or old age, they are not trying to board up the windows and keep the light out and meditate on the "good" alone. They don't do that.

We have among us a lot of people who have made a doctrine out of saying that everybody should think good thoughts all the time. That is like saying one school of painting is the only school. These people are taking up a position in the pink fluff, and they are trying to get you in there too, where the cotton candy sticks to you.

Then we have the tough-minded types who think that only some kind of Marxism is going to save the world from the fat cats — not even knowing that the fat cats ran Russia, that the Christmas on Earth concept of the Christians and the Communists is, in those hands, only a simulated version of the real thing, designed at the core to make people passive and live a slave's life.

David Icke is not interested in settling for a soft version of the truth, and so he keeps traveling around the world and speaking to larger audiences.

David knows that we have somehow taken on the work of building a vast Machine, and this Machine dispenses one reality that comes down and casts the main vote for the main way that life is heading along into the future. It isn't just a box in the sky that hypnotizes everybody. It's more like a pyramid, and we have helped out down at the bottom with the boards and the blocks in the dust and the shapes of our own trance. He doesn't buy into the Machine, and he is telling people about it, and they are listening. That is what's going on.

Yes, there are details, and we talk about those in this interview, and you will read that. There are lots of details, more in his own books. But what's going on is a man looking at the Machine and giving his description of it. You may see it from a different angle but it's the same Machine, and when you hear David talk about it, you'll wake up. It's the same Machine. We have it here in front of us. We're busy taking care of it and making it a good Machine and all the rest of it, but when we start to hear how it really works and what the result of that is, then we stir in our dreams and we begin to open our eyes and see something new. Yes, there is something new out there. We don't have to end up with old myths and the old gods and the old pre-praised dreams. There is a lot of room for something else.

I could say a lot more, but you get the idea. I know you do. Here is a man who is not afraid to talk about what he sees, the Machine and the new day and night that lie past it. Hear how he talks and you'll find something out. You will.

You won't agree with everything. There will be stretches where you'll say, no, that's wrong, that can't be, that's impossible, how could he imagine that ... and then while you're saying this over and over like a mantra you'll be reading more and you'll find yourself saying, What? What did he say? Oh my God. And you'll keep reading and the tune will change and you'll be right in there with it, discovering something you never knew before but seemed to believe already. Bingo bango. You'll be right there in the car going two hundred miles an hour with him. So go ahead, take the ride.

Jon Rappoport
San Diego, California
1998

Diana:
Murdered by the Brotherhood?

Jon Rappoport (JR): I was told that because Princess Diana was going to marry Fayed, and he was Muslim, she was already reading the Koran. She was thinking of converting. So imagine having one of her sons become the King. His mother is a Muslim. Where could this go?

David Icke (DI): With Diana there are so many unanswered questions. I don't believe the crash was an accident. The French "investigation" into her death has been a farce and quite clearly designed to lead nowhere. They allowed months to pass until memory of the crash began to fade as other stories took the headlines. Then, as quietly as possible, they announced the inquiry was being closed without establishing what happened. It took the same form as the equally farcical cover-up of the TWA 800 crash over New York.

They don't want to find the truth because those manipulating these inquiries already know what it is. Why else would they turn down an offer from experts at Mercedes to examine Diana's car? Why were the parents of the driver, Henri Paul, refused a second postmortem? Because an independent examination would expose the official lies and deceit. Henri Paul wasn't drunk, as video pictures at the Ritz Hotel clearly show before he drove the car. Injecting drugs which produce alcohol in the blood is child's play and so is tampering with samples.

As I'll talk about later, the potential for mind-controlling people, drivers and others, is simply immense. Paul and even the Paparazzi — much as I deplore their methods — were the scapegoats, the patsies, to take the blame for what others did. The first reports after the crash said that Diana's condition was "not catastrophic." But the ambulance team took an hour and a half to get her to hospital and even when they did move her, the ambulance driver was told to drive at no more than 25 miles an hour. They stopped the ambulance again within walking distance of the hospital after ignoring three other hospitals that were closer. Diana once said: "One day I'm going in a helicopter and it'll blow up. MI-5 will do away with me." I'm sure she was very close to the truth with that statement.

A contact on the fringes of the British Intelligence told me how easy it was to set up a crash, but he said that you couldn't be certain that the target would die on impact. So, he said, you make sure the emergency team includes people working for you and the patient is then certain not to survive. My intuition tells me that something like that happened, but there is a lot more investigation to be done.

It was immensely convenient that she died when she did, just at a time when she was coming into her power. She was starting to take on major worldwide issues. She had the ability to attract global publicity for any cause she picked up and ran with. She had moved on from purely health and psychological issues into landmines. She had highlighted that whole problem in a matter of months, globally, in a way that had never been done before.

I remember Henry Kissinger being interviewed after Diana died. He said she was diplomatically and politically uncontrollable. I think that is one major reason it was decided that she had to be terminated. Politicians, in particular the people involved in the global manipulation, like Kissinger, talk to each other via codes and symbols. So when Kissinger says she was diplomatically and politically uncontrollable, for me he is saying this is why she was terminated. Also, when someone is seen as a symbol for love and goodness, the elite Brotherhood often targets them to make the people despair and to break their spirit.

JR: In the political landscape, any time a person shows up who does have that power to immediately attract a large audience, and who is genuinely curious about what is going on in the world — all sorts of red lights begin flashing for political manipulators.

DI: Yes. That phrase, "diplomatically and politically uncontrollable," is their worst nightmare. They want to be able to operate behind a smokescreen of what you might call "normality." One version of

life is consistently conditioned into the mass con-
ciousness, while a totally different agenda is
unfolding behind that smokescreen. I think Diana
was beginning to stumble into it. So she was
extremely dangerous. Far more dangerous than
people with guns. For the manipulators, commu-
nication of what is really going on is the worst
nightmare. Words can open the eyes of people
who are currently caught in the headlights of an
oncoming car. The headlights are the massive conditioning imposed through the education system
and the media, etc., which has given us a totally
manipulated version of life, while another secret
agenda goes on behind it.

Anyone in the public arena who can begin to
open people's eyes to what is going on is a very
dangerous person. The more people who do it, of
course, the more holes are sprung in the dike, and
the quicker we dismantle this edifice of manipulation and control.

JR: Eventually they run out of fingers.

DI: If you look at Diana, she had instant global publicity for anything she picked up and ran
with. She certainly had a score to settle with the
British establishment and the House of Windsor.
She made that very clear. If she came out with any
hidden-agenda material concealed from the public, it would not be on the periphery anymore. In
England there was a magazine called Scallywag
which changed its name to Spiked. The magazine
named some famous business people and politicians in Britain as pedophiles and talked about the

way political manipulation went on behind the scenes. I do have it from a solid gold authority that at least for a time Mohammed Al Fayed funded that.

JR: That magazine?

DI: Yes. Diana would probably have had a bigger picture of what was going on from a number of sources. Of course the Al Fayed family were very close and related to the Saudi, Adnan Khashoggi, one of the most notorious arms dealers in the world. Diana was in the middle of a campaign against landmines, so there are a lot of questions to ask about her death on all sides. Khashoggi is an associate of George Bush, the former President. Bush, in turn, is a very close friend of Queen Elizabeth and Prince Philip. Makes you think. One thing is for sure, from my research, there's no way a "hit" on Diana could have been made by the British establishment without the Queen knowing about it beforehand. If we can expose the truth behind her murder, it will alert the world to what is really going on, and we will.

The Brotherhood Agenda

Jon Rappoport (JR): To go to the idea of an agenda behind the scenes, how specifically do you believe it is articulated and what is it? What are these people doing — I guess we could call them a global elite. What are they trying for, what is their timetable, and how far do you think they are willing to go to get what they want?

David Icke (DI): The agenda is to impose the centralized control of the world and to create a population of human robots. We are seriously closing in on that. In fact, humanity in general has long been solidifying mentally and emotionally into automatons.

JR: Where does the conspiracy come in?

DI: In three major ways,

One: conspiring to remove people and organizations that are a threat to that agenda.

Two: conspiring to put into positions of economic and political power people who will make that agenda a reality by legislation. For example, Clinton and Bush are not opponents but associates, members of the same organizations, working toward the same goals. I have documented that in my book titled "... and the truth shall set you free"

(Bridge of Love, 1997).

Three: orchestrating events like Oklahoma City, like Waco, like the world wars, to manipulate public opinion into demanding that the agenda becomes a reality. I call this Problem-Reaction-Solution.

It works by creating the problem, getting the public reaction "something must be done, this can't go on, what are they going to do about it," and then the people who have created the problem and stimulated that reaction offer the solution to the problems they have created. Oklahoma is a classic example.

What would normally be opposed by large numbers of people is suddenly demanded by them. Further erosion of basic freedoms is not on the surface a popular policy. But Problem-Reaction-Solution so manipulates the mass psyche that people demand "solutions" which they would normally reject.

Who would normally pressure the government into giving more power to the security agencies to tap phones, stop and search, or enter homes without permission? No one. But if you plant a "terrorist bomb," the public clamors for more stringent laws. They give the government, the police, and the security services more power. They are building a fascist world this way.

In Britain we've got cameras in the streets all over the place now and people are demanding that it expand to their area. In a place called Chippenham in Wiltshire I read that some local people are having charity sales to raise the money to pay for cameras in the streets. They are actually raising money to take their own freedoms away.

So these are the three main areas of conspiracy:

(1) Removing any threat to the agenda, which can mean removing politicians, assassinations, or discrediting organizations which are exposing what is going on;

(2) Putting people into power who will make the agenda happen; and

(3) Creating events that will get the public to demand it happens.

Those three things are the conspiracy, but they are conspiracies to introduce the agenda. It's the agenda that is the foundation. It's been going on for thousands of years. We've reached the point now in this unfolding story where you don't really have to look ahead and say, well, it looks like this is going to happen. You just turn on the news, and it's unfolding before your eyes every day.

It is very interesting to ask the question "who benefits" when these events happen. Who benefits from them happening and who benefits from us believing the media's version of what happened?

JR: Who benefited from Oklahoma City?

DI: Not the people who died, not their parents and loved ones, not the city. No one benefited except those who wished to increase the power of law enforcement agencies in America. Those who wish to further erode basic freedoms and disempower the American psyche with even more fear. Within 24 hours of that bomb Bill Clinton was calling for an easing of restrictions on the military's involvement in domestic law enforcement. Antiterrorism bills have gone through Congress purely as a result of the bombing, and they went through on the nod with some Congressmen terrified of even saying a word against them because of the fierce public reaction they would have attracted. So it was a frame-up which allowed further freedoms to be eroded.

I'm not saying those prosecuted for the bombing were not involved at all — I don't know that — but to say that they organized it is simply ludicrous. As some explosives experts have said in the alternative media, the fuel-fertilizer bomb in the Ryder truck could not possibly have caused that scale of damage.

Retired Brigadier General Ben Partin, who spent much of his military career in explosives, has said that charges placed on pillars within the Murrah building were the only way such a pattern of damage could have been caused. Ted Gunderson, an FBI agent for 28 years, tells a similar story. He has established there were two, possibly three, explosions, by studying the readout of earthquake monitoring equipment at Oklahoma University. The smallest of them was the Ryder truck bomb designed to obscure the other ones going off.

And what about the parents of children who died in this horror who have established that agents of the Bureau of Alcohol, Tobacco, and Firearms were in full combat gear around the building long before the bomb went off? The official story is that the bomb was aimed at the BATF in the Murrah building as a protest for their involvement at Waco. How strange then that no BATF personnel were in the building when the bomb exploded!

JR: What is this "agenda" in detail?

DI: The structure of the agenda is a world government which would make all major decisions, a world currency which would be electronic, no cash — and there are massive implications for freedom in that — a world central bank and a world army. They are creating the world army by expanding NATO to encompass more and more countries until it becomes the world army by stealth. That is happening now, as anyone can see.

JR: You are talking about superstates and regions, larger than current nations.

DI: Under this world government would come three massive superstates. The European Union is the most advanced because it started back in the fifties. It began life as a free-trade area. "It's just about trade. Don't worry about it. It's all fine."

Over a period of time, another mind-controlling technique has been employed to evolve the "free trade" into what it was always meant to be. I call it the Stepping Stones Approach. You know where you are heading from the start, but if you introduce what you really want immediately, it's such a jump, such a change, that people say what's going on here, we're not having this.

So you first introduce what you can get away with. In Europe after the last war it was a free-trade area. It was sold to people this way: If we trade together in Europe, we will stop fighting with each other. But of course that's not true. You just fight in a different way, that's all.

Over a period of decades there has been a series of stepping stones, each of which has been projected to the public as totally unconnected to the others. Europe has "evolved" from a free-trade area into, now, a massive, centralized superstate where national law is every day overridden by European law made by bureaucrats in Brussels. As with NATO, the European Union is being expanded into Eastern Europe now that the manipulated "Cold War" is over.

JR: In America, you would have the case of the second superstate.

DI: In America, the agenda has been to do exactly the same. If the technique works, why change it? First of all, create a free-trade area. We have that now with NAFTA, the North American Free Trade Agreement taking in Canada, America and Mexico. This is planned to expand in the same way as Europe, into a centralized state for the whole of the Americas.

JR: And both the Democrats and the Republicans pushed NAFTA through with virtually identical speeches.

DI: George Bush, Republican, and Bill Clinton, Democrat, have made speeches saying they want to see the NAFTA free-trade area operate from the tip of North America to the tip of South America.

Bill Clinton was in South America in 1997 saying exactly this — we want the Americas to come together, we are one people. He bolsters this by asserting that, when the Spaniards and the Europeans came to the Americas, they didn't see the Americas as different areas, it was one. This is all "newspeak" and "elitespeak" that echoes and re-echoes as they now begin to evolve the agenda of NAFTA in exactly the way they have in Europe — into a superstate with centralized control of the whole of the Americas. This includes a plan to break up Canada, which I will detail in my next book, The Biggest Secret.

JR: When you lay it on the table and look at it, it's not a happy prospect. It isn't real community they're talking about.

DI: No. In 1994 there was another free-trade area created, this time in Asia-Australia. Again Bill Clinton was at the launch. It's called APEC, Asia Pacific Economic Cooperation. That's designed to be evolved in the same way into the Pacific Union. The Asia-Australian version of the European Union and the American Union.

Then under that edifice of control, the World Government and the Superstates, would come nation states and regions with virtually no power whatsoever. The agenda is to deunify any response to the edifice of power above, which is why the plan is to break up nation states into regions. It is being done in a very subtle way because it is all about mind manipulation and emotional manipulation. Only by that means can the few control billions.

The Origin of the Brotherhood

Jon Rappoport (JR): Earlier you referred to an ancient root for this kind of strategy.

David Icke (DI): I think we are experiencing Atlantis revisited. I have been very surprised at the amount of three-dimensional evidence there is, geological, biological, to show that the so-called mythical continent of Atlantis did exist on what is now called the Mid-Atlantic Ridge. The terrain under the ocean there fits Plato's description of what Atlantis looked like, and this is one of the most active volcanic regions on the planet. Great areas of land which are now the seabed around the Azores were above the surface between 11,000 and 13,000 years ago. Walls and pyramids have been identified under the water in the region where Atlantis is supposed to have been and I will be presenting some detailed evidence for the existence of Atlantis in my next book. All along the Atlantic coasts of the Americas, Europe, and Africa, you find the same stories and legends of the lost land, a disappearing continent, and the "white gods" from there coming out of the sea bringing amazing knowledge.

JR: What kind of knowledge?

DI: The understanding of sound and magnetics which allowed them to move colossal pieces of rock by making them weightless. Conventional history and geology have always found it impossible to explain how the fantastic structures of the ancient world were built by so-called "primitive" people. For instance at Baalbek in Lebanon there are three rocks called the Trilithon, each weighing 800 tons, which the ancients moved at least a third of a mile and then placed in a wall 20 feet off the ground.

How did they do that without very advanced knowledge? That's only one of scores of examples all over the world. Look at the Great Pyramid at Giza. We still could not build that today with conventional technology. The precision of these structures was so tight and the way the rocks were cut was so perfect that we are certainly not dealing with a "primitive" people. There were two levels of people, the masses who did not have the knowledge, and the few who were initiated through the temple or "Mystery Schools" in Atlantis.

I have no doubt that this knowledge was brought originally from extraterrestrial sources and probably with quite positive intent. This was the "Golden Age" of native legend all over the world. The extraterrestrials lived openly among the people and these became the "gods" of ancient legend.

The word the Old Testament translates as "God," singular, comes from words like Elohim and others which mean "gods," plural. But either some of these extraterrestrials began to lose it or another group came in, because the knowledge began to be abused. Knowledge is neutral. It's not the knowledge that is positive or negative, it is the use of it. Here they had knowledge not only of magnetics, but also how to manipulate energy fields and the minds of people.

There developed two secret networks passing on the knowledge via initiation, the "white magicians" as some people call them, and the "black magicians" who used it to manipulate and control. I will call the latter the Brotherhood. I merely mean those who have abused the knowledge in their desire to control and dominate. My research continues, but my feeling is that this Brotherhood is connected to the malevolent extraterrestrials who arrived to end the "Golden Age" and cause mayhem and destruction.

Cleverness without wisdom is one of the most destructive forces you can experience, and cleverness without love is the most destructive of all. That is what we are dealing with here. I think Atlantis already had an empire which went into Europe and North Africa and when Atlantis was going down a lot of the white and black magicians left and started again in these other centers, especially Egypt and Sumer.

I will give you a quote from Manly P. Hall, the Freemasonic historian, which I found in his superb book called, The Secret Teachings of All Ages.*

---

* Los Angeles: Philosophical Research, 1978.

He wrote:

> "While the elaborate ceremonial magic of antiquity was not necessarily evil, there arose from its perversion several false schools of sorcery or black magic ... [in Egypt] ... the black magicians of Atlantis continued to exercise superhuman powers until they had completely undermined and corrupted the morals of the primitive Mysteries ... they usurped the position formerly occupied by the initiates, and seized the reins of spiritual government."

That Brotherhood is the same Brotherhood that controls the world today through the banking, business, political and "legal" systems it created, and by manipulating and conditioning the minds of the people through the "education" system and the media.

Working behind the scenes all the way through has been this malevolent extraterrestrial group which is seeking to take over the planet through its human elite while the people have no idea what is going on. Therefore, there must be a reason why they cannot just take it over by force. I think one reason is that there have never been that many of them. Other extraterrestrial races, I believe, are seeking to help humanity to wake up, but they won't override our free will, while the malevolent group have no problem with that.

So when we are manipulated to fear some extraterrestrial invasion from space, they are trying to make us look in the wrong direction. The extraterrestrials working through the Brotherhood are not going to invade from space. They are already here. They have been from the start of all this.

If you look at what's happening today, at the fact that secret science is light years in advance of what we are allowed to see in the public arena, you see that the elite, who are at the cutting edge of that science and the technological potential it offers, have once again the ability to cause mayhem on the planet and great destruction.

JR: Conventional history has great civilizations like Egypt and Sumer spontaneously appearing out of nothing.

DI: We know most civilizations evolve over a period of time to great advancement. If a society appears already advanced at the start, it must have been caused by some sudden influx of knowledge. I think this Atlantean knowledge was responsible for creating those civilizations and that ultimately that knowledge came in from extraterrestrial sources. People who are genuinely researching Egypt from an open-minded point of view, are suggesting that the Sphinx in Egypt was built per- haps as far back as 10,500 B.C., in the window of time that followed the destruction of Atlantis around 11,000 B.C.

Stealing the Knowledge

Jon Rappoport (JR): How would you approach certain fundamental Christians who are on to aspects of political manipulation in America? They then say the Earth is five or six thousand years old. They can't get past that.

David Icke (DI): I would start off by saying again that there is no such thing as good or bad knowledge. There is not. There is just the positive and negative use of it. If you are going to write off what we might call ancient esoteric knowledge as "of the devil" and throw the baby out with the bathwater, you are actually helping to suppress the very knowledge that we need to understand.

There were mystery schools, what we would call secret societies, that were set up in the ancient world to pass on this knowledge to people they thought would use it with integrity. But when you start to research history there was also a structure set up by what I call the Brotherhood. These were the black magicians of Atlantis, connected to extraterrestrial groups, who wished to take over the planet. There were not enough of them to do it openly and so they began the agenda to do it by manipulating the human mind and emotions, by putting people in mental prisons.

JR: The agenda of more and more centralized control over people's lives and minds.

DI: Yes. I think two things have happened over the last several thousand years, particularly from around 3,000 B.C. in ancient Sumer, what we now call Iraq. The Brotherhood's structure of control has expanded and become more and more sophisticated and they have infiltrated and taken over the secret networks that began with a more positive intent. This has ensured that knowledge is given only to the people they want to have it.

At the same time this same force, the Brotherhood, has set up institutions in the public arena like the Roman Church, Judaism, Hinduism, and Islam, to suck this advanced esoteric knowledge out of the public domain so it is hoarded in their hands only. So if you look at the Inquisition in Europe, the Inquisition made it suicidal to even talk about this esoteric knowledge. You were a devil. You were a witch. It sucked the knowledge out of the public domain.

The Brotherhood took control of Europe from the start, as I will document in great detail in The Biggest Secret. Eventually, it centered itself in the British Isles and London. This is why those little islands built an empire which spanned the world. And what happened as the British and European white races expanded into the Americas, Africa, the Middle East, Asia, Australia, and New Zealand? They destroyed the native peoples and cultures and took the ancient esoteric knowledge and the true history of the world out of circulation. That is what the mass burning of books and texts was done for. They wanted to create a year Zero and erase all knowledge of who we are and where we came from. One of the most horrendous examples of this was the burning of the Great Library at Alexandria in the 5th century, when thousands of priceless texts from all over the ancient world were destroyed.

JR: It also imposed a very rigid belief system based on the Bible, which of course has been changed and rewritten so many times.

DI: The King James Version of the Bible, which has been the master copy for Christianity in the more modern world, was shown in a survey done in 1881 to have 36,191 translation errors alone. And the Bible texts are written in the esoteric code of the Mystery Schools. Initiates know what they really mean, but the people are told to take them literally.

Christianity has been used as a front for the Brotherhood to hide behind. In France and down into Jerusalem at the time of the Crusades a secret society called the Knights Templar was formed. They said they were protecting pilgrims going on pilgrimages to Jerusalem. But they never did that. For many years after their formation there were only nine of them! That doesn't protect many pilgrims.

What they did, however, was move into a building right next to the Temple Mount where the Al-Aksa Mosque is today. It is said that Solomon's temple was on this site and Herod's temple and various other ancient religious temples. I will show in The Biggest Secret, however, that Solomon's Temple and Solomon himself were symbolic and not literal.

Anyway, after a few years of studying and searching under that site, they would seem to have found something significant. They were certainly a secret society that had access to the Egyptian, Atlantean knowledge which was being passed down, and they suddenly started expanding very rapidly from nine knights to hundreds and more.

They have virtually been written out of conventional history. There is just a mention here and a mention there as if they are not important. When you look at the true history, they were, in fact, rivaling the Roman Church both for power and for wealth. To join the Templars you had to give over all your wealth to them. They were signing up many of the noble families of Europe and taking their land and their wealth and all that they had. The Templars must have had some serious knowledge to attract that scale of commitment.

They became immensely wealthy. They had massive centers in Paris and London and other places. They had the crowned heads in Europe up to their necks in debt to them. They were in effect the Crusade-period version of the Federal Reserve, the privately owned "central bank" which controls the United States. They had a massive fleet of ships quite capable of crossing the Atlantic. They collected the taxation at one time in Britain and they owned great areas of land.

Where the central lawcourts in Britain are today, where all the barristers have their Inner Temples, etc., that's Templar land. It's called Temple Bar in London. Now I'm not saying that all Templars were negative. These organizations are structured as compartmentalized pyramids. Many — even most — of their initiates can be of positive intent, but they are only allowed to know what they need to know.

The real power is at the top, which decides who progresses up the levels of knowledge and how much they will be told. If you look at what the Templars did, however, the outcomes of their actions, no one will persuade me they have been supporting human freedom. They have played a major role in creating the structure of control, financially and politically, we have today. So have their fellow "Knights," the Knights Hospitaller of St. John of Jerusalem, also known as the Knights of Malta. They have initiates in positions of power throughout the world.

JR: King Philip was not the Templars' friend.

DI: In 1307 the King of France, Philip the Fair, a guy who was up to his neck in debt, decided he wanted to get rid of the Templars and therefore get rid of his debt. He also wanted the money they had. So he had secret orders sent to his military chiefs across France to arrest all Templars.

The pope, a puppet of Philip, supported him. The arrests happened on Friday the 13th, which is why Friday the 13th has been held to be unlucky ever since. Philip the Fair obviously had light hair,

because fair certainly did not describe his de-
meanor. Many of the Templars were arrested, but
a large number got away. When Philip and his
henchmen marched into the Templar headquarters in Paris to pick up the loot there was none
there. The Templar fleet of ships has never been
found and their loot has never been found. What
happened to them?

JR: The Templars became a quite powerful
"financial services" outfit.

DI: By this time, the 12-1300s, the Knights
Templar had in fact already established the structure of the modern banking system which controls
the world today, the system of lending people
money that does not exist and charging interest
on it. When they were purged in France in 1307,
they were accused of what we would call today
satanic ritual abuse, murder and sacrifice of adults
and particularly children.

People will say, oh, those confessions were
obtained under torture, and some of them were,
but they correlated with what other people said
without being tortured.

And when you do the research in the modern
world you find that the people now at the peak of
the pyramid of power are also involved in the
ritual murder and abuse of children. These are the
successors to the Templars economically and politically. I think that is a coincidence not to be dismissed lightly.

Again, I'm not saying that all Templars did this,
only the ones who were using that organization

as a vehicle for the Brotherhood. Also, interestingly, one of the Knights Templar policies or ambitions right back in the 12-1300s was to create a United States of Europe, which is what they've done via their other masks in the years that have followed.

One of the places the Templars went in their ships to get away from the purge in France was Portugal. There they operated behind a Christian front organization called the Knights of Christ. The Knights of Christ were the Templars under another name. They were a maritime organization. Their Grand Master was Prince Henry the Navigator, the famous explorer. They had maps of the world which conventional history even today denies exist, but people like Charles Hapgood, an American, and others, have found some of them.

These maps, drawn in that period, or available in that period, show areas of land mapped on the planet which, according to conventional history, Europeans did not know existed at that time. They knew the Americas were here. Of course they did. Columbus was far from the first European to come to America. I have a copy of the so-called Zeno Map which shows Greenland before it was covered in ice! There is also the map drawn in 1513 by the Turkish admiral Piri Reis, which shows what the landmass looks like under the Antarctic. In 1513, as now, it was a mile thick under ice, so how did he do it? He drew his map from ancient ones which went back thousands of years.

The Templars calling themselves the Knights of

Christ had some of those maps and one of the captains working with Prince Henry the Navigator was the father-in-law of Christopher Columbus! Christopher Columbus knew what he was looking for. The idea that he thought he was sailing to India and tripped over the Americas is the smokescreen to stop us asking how he knew. The symbol of the Knights Templar was the red cross on the white background. The flags that Columbus flew on his ships when he came to "discover" the Americas had the red cross on the white background, because that was a Templar expedition and they knew what they were going to find because they had been there before.

I'll give you an example of how prearranged and organized this European takeover of the Americas really was. When the Spaniard Cortez followed Columbus to Central America, he and his small group controlled the place very quickly. There's no way this could have happened if the native tribes had fiercely resisted. But they had an ancient belief that their white god, Quetzalcoatl, was going to return in 1519 wearing feathers and holding a cross.

They called Quetzalcoatl the "Plumed Serpent." Cortez arrived in 1519 wearing feathers and holding a cross!!! As a result, the native people thought Quetzalcoatl had returned and the Spanish were well established before the native people realized their mistake. The Brotherhood knew the native belief and used it to their advantage. It was all calculated and organized well in advance.

Also, conventional history does not connect

Columbus with John Cabot who sailed from the key Templar port of Bristol, England, to "discover" North America four or five years after the Columbus voyage. But as the Freemasonic historian Manly P. Hall has pointed out, Cabot (real name Giovanni Caboto) and Columbus both lived in Genoa, Italy, at the same time and were connected to the same secret society network. Genoa, Venice and Northern Italy were and are a major center for the Brotherhood wing known as the Black Nobility. A coincidence? Of course not.

The Black Nobility took over England with the arrival on the throne of their frontman, William of Orange, in 1688. They made the City of London the world financial center after William signed the charter to create the Bank of England in 1694. They went on to build the British Empire. The empire was not, in truth, "British." It was the empire of the Black Nobility based in Britain.

JR: Where else did the Templar fleet go?

DI: One of the key families behind the creation of the Templars was a French family called St. Clair — a name which has evolved into the Scottish name Sinclair. The St. Clairs owned great chunks of land in Scotland. They were one of the major Scottish families. They owned land just south of Edinburgh and there they built a church called Rosslyn Chapel. I've been to it. In the stonework of Rosslyn Chapel are cactus plants and sweetcorn plants that were only found in America. That chapel and that stonework were built before Columbus left on his journey.

There is a book available called Prince Henry Sinclair: His Expedition to the New World,* a voyage which took place a hundred years before Columbus went on his. So they knew the Americas were here. After the French purge in 1307 one group of Templars went around the west coast of Ireland and Scotland. There were many reasons for this. They had great friends in Scotland and Brotherhood blood families were there, like the St. Clairs and others. And at that time Scotland was excommunicated by the Pope, so his "Destroy the Templars" order did not apply, at least for while.

The Templars went to Scotland and later re-emerged behind another mask. They called themselves the Scottish Rite of Freemasonry. The most all-pervading rite of Freemasonry in the world today, which manipulates world politics, world business, world banking, etc., is called the Scottish Rite because that is where the Templars went after the purge.

Again we see another mask on the same face winding its way through history. If you look at the background to the people who have turned Europe into the superstate, the United States of Europe the Templars wanted all those centuries ago, you are looking at members of the Scottish Rite of Freemasonry and its offshoots. In other words the Templars and the Brotherhood network have got what they always intended to get. They just used another name.

---

* By Frederick J. Pohl (Nimbus Publishing Ltd., 1997).

Why the United States Has NEVER Been Free

Jon Rappoport (JR): Now we come to the immigration of Europeans into America.

David Icke (DI): The people who were behind that influx, particularly from Britain, were leading initiates of the secret society network, people like Sir Francis Bacon. He was a Templar and the top Rosicrucian in Britain. He was carrying out the long-term agenda of the Black Nobility-Brotherhood which had based itself in the British Isles.

Take that American hero, Benjamin Franklin. He was the Henry Kissinger of his day. I know I'm going to upset people who look at the Founding Fathers with rose-colored glasses and think they all stood for human freedom. But I don't think America's ever been free of control from Europe and especially Britain and the Black Nobility.

Benjamin Franklin was the leading Freemason in Philadelphia where the whole thing was organized from. He was a high initiate of the French secret society network, including the Nine Sisters Lodge. This organization was one of those behind the orchestration of the French Revolution. He was also a leading member of secret societies in

Britain, including a satanic, blood-drinking secret society known as the Hell Fire Club, peopled by some of the leading politicians and businessmen and members of royalty in Britain.

So here you had a man in Benjamin Franklin who had a foot in each camp, in the American colonies, in Britain and in France at the time of the Revolution. This is why so many Frenchmen — Freemasons — were involved with the American War of Independence.

JR: Your position is that the American Revolution was manipulated, staged. That it really was not about freedom. There were other motives.

DI: There was agitation for the American colonies to demand their freedom. But there was one force playing two sides off against each other to create a desired outcome. In Britain you had the Brotherhood elite who had, among their front men and subordinates, people who were controlling King George III, who was himself a Brotherhood initiate. He was a Hanover, the same "royal" bloodline as the Windsors.

The Brotherhood started a war between Britain and France, to create tremendous economic problems. The King of England had to raise more money. Those same advisors then told King George that a great way of getting the money without opposition from his subjects at home would be to impose more taxation on the American colonies. At the same time the henchmen for this same Brotherhood elite in the colonies began agitating the people there to rebel against these [taxation] policies arranged by their British arm. Eventually this agitation built up to the point where the King withdrew most of the taxation, but it was too late.

JR: You're saying the elite didn't want this pressure stopped?

DI: Yes. We come to the Boston Tea Party. Official history tells us that your average American colonists dressed up like Mohawk Indians took tea from a ship called the Dartmouth, and threw it into Boston Harbor, to protest against the system which allowed the East India Company, a front for the British Crown, to undercut American suppliers of tea.

If you look at sources like the Freemasonic historian Manly P. Hall, you get a very different version of the story. Hall points out that these tea-tossing "Indians" were members of the St. Andrews Freemasonry lodge in Boston, and he names them. They were led by their junior warden, Paul Revere. We would call what they did today a photo opportunity. It was all part of the plan to fan the flames of rebellion to ensure that the momentum for revolution was increased.

JR: Once the War began, didn't the British fight to win?

DI: The British generals did everything they could to lose. Key people behind the Colonial armies and the key people leading the British Army were all Freemasons, especially the Scottish Rite of Freemasonry. As Manly P. Hall says, of the 56 signatories of the American Declaration of Independence, almost 50 were known Freemasons, and only one was known not to be. In other words, this hidden hand, which can be charted through apparently unconnected historical events, has been working through all sides to a common agenda.

That is not to say that every Freemason is involved in this. Certainly not. Quite the opposite is true. The vast majority have no idea what that Secret Society is being used for. They are kept in the dark and fed bullshit. The mushroom technique. Since the American War of Independence, the United States has been controlled by the Brotherhood and a number of their bloodlines have been elected to the White House.

Signs and Symbols of "Brotherhood" America

Jon Rappoport (JR): You've spoken and written about little oddities in the structure of Washington, D.C.

David Icke (DI): If you look at the street plan of Washington, D.C. — and there are some books that do this — you find esoteric symbols, buildings and road layouts all built according to the sacred geometry of Freemasonry and the ancient Mystery Schools which spawned the Brotherhood. You have streets crossing at angles of 33 degrees and there are occult pentagrams in the street plan.

The pentagram, or five-pointed star, is not a negative symbol in its original form, but the Brotherhood turns it upside down to symbolize the negative, the malevolent. The points of reversed pentagrams go directly into both the White House and the Congress building. The center of a pentagram is a pentagon and so you have the headquarters of the United States military called the Pentagon, and shaped as that symbol.

Congress is called Capitol Hill after Capitoline Hill, a Sacred place of the Brotherhood during the days of the Roman Empire. It's no surprise, therefore, that Madeleine Albright, a member of the Brotherhood, should make a pilgrimage to Capitoline Hill on her first official visit to Italy as Secretary of State. Congress is not a political building. It is a temple to the Brotherhood. The obelisk is an ancient symbol of the phallic going back to Egypt and beyond. Hence the Washington Monument is a massive obelisk. Everything is energy, and symbols affect the energy field and speak to our subconscious. We are being manipulated without knowing it.

It's remarkable to see it when this is pointed out, the patterns, the pentagrams, the triangles. This knowledge and the same symbols can be identified thousands of years ago, and they are still used today because of the way they affect the human subconscious mind and as symbols of Brotherhood control. The most blatant one is the pyramid and all-seeing eye on the dollar bill, a symbol of the Brotherhood wing called the Bavarian Illuminati which was officially formed on May 1st, 1776.

The national flags and logos of the major corporations consist of ancient esoteric symbols, too, because they are owned by the same Brotherhood. They are laughing at the masses because the truth is in front of their eyes, but without access to the suppressed knowledge, they can't see it.

If you go a few minutes' drive from the White House you'll find a remarkable building in Washington which sums up what I've been talking about here. It is basically an Egyptian temple. It is a big building with two sphinx outside. Behind the pillars at the front is a massive depiction of the rising sun. The Brotherhood use the Sun as their symbol, as they have since they were formed. They understand the true nature and power of the Sun and how to harness its immense outpourings of magnetic solar energy.

This building, this Egyptian temple in the center of Washington, D.C., is the supreme headquarters, 33rd degree, of the Scottish Rite of Freemasonry. These people, the elite, have an obsession about following the rituals they have inherited from the ancient world. They are following the rituals of the black magicians of Atlantis. In fact, through reincarnation, at least some of them are the black magicians of Atlantis.

Talking of rituals, it is no accident that the Kennedy assassination was performed as a ritual killing of a Sun King. Nor that the place where Diana's car crashed in Paris was an ancient pagan sacrificial site. I will be explaining this in detail in The Biggest Secret.

Another of their symbols is the lighted torch. So you have the Statue of Liberty holding the torch of the Brotherhood, the "Illuminati," and around her head is the spiked halo, an ancient depiction of the rays of the Sun. The Statue of Liberty was given to New York by, wait for it, the French Freemasons.

The Olympic torch is the same. They control the Olympics and where it goes according to their agenda. Atlanta is one of their goddess symbols. She was said to be the best athlete in Calcydon and was suckled by Artemis herself, another of their goddesses. Where was the centennial Olympics held? Not in Greece where you would have thought, but in Atlanta.

One of the inner groups manipulating the creation of the United States from its headquarters in Britain was called the Columbian Faction, after an ancient goddess called Columba, a name for the negative, destructive, aspect of goddess Aphrodite. The Romans called this aspect of Aphrodite, Venus Columba, which means Venus the Dove. Many times you see the dove in Brotherhood symbolism. To the uninitiated it stands for "peace," but in truth it symbolizes the goddess Columba.

This is why we have Washington in the District of Columbia. This is why we have British Columbia, Columbia University, Columbia Broadcasting (CBS), and Columbia Pictures. And what is the symbol of Columbia Pictures? A lady holding a lighted torch! What is the logo of Columbia University? A lighted torch! And the logo of CBS is the (All-Seeing) eye. This is also the true meaning of the name Columbus. He usually signed his name Colon. Columbus was a Brotherhood name symbolizing the goddess, Columba. Now you know why.

The Brotherhood killed John F. Kennedy and what did they put on his grave? Their "eternal flame." In Dallas after the killing, the Freemasons built an obelisk near the site and on the top is a flaming torch.

The Brotherhood is headquartered in Britain, particularly the financial center, in the Square Mile known as the "City" of London, and that's where the United States is really controlled from.

I think we are at the point now of Atlantis revisited, where the people of the world have a massive opportunity to make a different choice. Instead of allowing the few to control the show by giving our power away, as people did at the end of Atlantis, we have the chance now to take our power back and break this cycle once and for all, to go in a different direction.

The Brotherhood Pyramid

Jon Rappoport (JR): What does this "Templar" secret-society structure look like today?

David Icke (DI): The web of the Brotherhood is very complex today with endless offshoots and connecting organizations, but its basic structure is very simple. It is based on pyramids within pyramids, like Russian dolls.

The peak of each individual network fuses into one collective peak, the top of the global pyramid, and there sit the leading black magicians, adepts, and bloodlines, who administer the agenda on behalf of the extraterrestrials. At this level all the banks, transnationals, news media, secret societies, security agencies, religions, etc., are the same organization working to the same agenda, although they may squabble with each other a lot. They are like bank robbers who agree on the job, but argue over how the spoils are to be shared out. Rule is by fear.

One of the most significant networks within the web is arranged around a secret society called the Round Table which was set up in Britain (the Brotherhood headquarters) in the latter part of the 19th century. Its front man was Cecil Rhodes, the guy who exploited Africa mercilessly with Rothschild money. Rhodesia was named after him. The Round Table helped to orchestrate the First World War and then began to create offshoot organizations working as one unit, but with different roles.

The first was the Royal Institute of International Affairs, based at Chatham House in London, which began in 1920. A year later came the Council on Foreign Relations in the United States, then came the Bilderberg Group in 1954, and the Trilateral Commission in 1972. These have among their number the top people in global banking, business, politics, the military, the media, education, and other institutions which control the planet. The Brotherhood manipulates its people, or its stooges, into positions of apparent power in all these areas and this is why you find so many pedophiles, satanists, and ritual killers in the so-called upper levels of society. It's structured to be that way. Anyone not playing the game is filtered out before they reach a significant level.

Virtually every president since 1921 has been a member of the Council on Foreign Relations along with Secretaries of State, heads of the armed forces, leaders in education, foreign ambassadors, editors, journalists, national news anchors. On and on it goes.

No matter what party is theoretically in power, the same story can be told. The administrations of Ford, Carter, Reagan, Bush, and Clinton have been awash from top to bottom with members of these organizations which answer in the end to a single leadership and a single agenda. Bill Clinton, Madeleine Albright (his Secretary of State), Colin Powell (the head of the armed forces at the time of the Gulf War), George Bush (who caused the Gulf War against his associate — yes, his associate — Saddam Hussein), are all connected to this network.

I expose all this in great detail in "... and the truth shall set you free," but let me give you an idea of its scope. Let us take the Bilderberg Group alone. It was officially launched at the Hotel Bilderberg in Oosterbeek, the Netherlands, in 1954, and involves the royal families of Europe as well as the heads of many other cherished institutions. Most people have never heard of this organization, and yet look at its frontmen!

The last five Secretary-Generals of NATO, Joseph Luns, Lord Carrington, Manfred Worner, Willy Claes, and Javier Solana, have been Bilderbergers and many more before them. So is the head of the World Bank, James Wolfenson, the head of the U.S. Federal Reserve, Alan Greenspan, the first two heads of the World Trade Organization, Peter D. Sutherland of Ireland, and Renato Ruggiero of Italy.

The head of the European Commission, Jacques Santer, is a Bilderberger. He is orchestrating the creation of the European Superstate with a single bank and currency, and virtually every major politician involved in doing the same; for example, Chancellor Kohl of Germany, the former British Prime Minister, Ted Heath, and the present one, Tony Blair, are Bilderberg attendees.

The Bosnian war was a manipulated conflict to advance the agenda of the NATO world army under Problem-Reaction-Solution. The more the horrors were broadcast on our television screens while the UN peacekeeping force looked ineffective, the louder came the global clamor that "something must be done." This allowed those who had caused the war to offer a solution to it — a 60,000 strong world army, the biggest multi-national force assembled since the Second World War. Now look at the common themes among all the major peace negotiators in Bosnia from the very start of that conflict.

Negotiators appointed by the European Union were Lord Carrington, chairman of the Bilderberg Group since 1991, president of the Royal Institute of International Affairs, and Trilateral Commission member. He was replaced by another British politician, Lord David Owen (Bilderberg Group, Trilateral Commission), and then came Carl Bildt, the former Swedish prime minister (Bilderberg Group). The United Nations-appointed negotiators were Cyrus Vance (Bilderberg Group, Council on Foreign Relations, Trilateral Commission), and a Norwegian, Thorvald Stoltenberg (Bilderberg Group, Trilateral Commission).

When they failed to achieve peace, along came an "independent" peace negotiator, Jimmy Carter, the first Trilateral Commission President of the United States, and Council on Foreign Relations member. Next came Bill Clinton's peace negotiator, Richard Holbrooke (Bilderberg Group, Trilateral Commission, Council on Foreign Relations), who negotiated the Dayton Agreement which installed the world army. The Defense Secretary was William Perry (Bilderberg Group), the Secretary of State was Warren Christopher (Council on Foreign Relations, Trilateral Commission) and the U.S. ambassador to the former Yugoslavia was Warren Zimmerman (Trilateral Commission, Council on Foreign Relations).

They all answered to the President, Bill Clinton (Bilderberg Group, Trilateral Commission, Council on Foreign Relations), who answered to the unelected David Rockefeller, the leading executive of the Bilderberg Group, Council on Foreign Relations and Trilateral Commission. The first head of the world army in Bosnia was Admiral Leighton Smith (Council on Foreign Relations), and the civilian operation was headed by Carl Bildt (Bilderberg Group).

Then look at the media and people like the owner, at least officially, of the Washington Post. She is Katharine Graham (Bilderberg Group, Trilateral Commission and Council on Foreign Relations). The Los Angeles Times, New York Times, Wall Street Journal and all the U.S. television networks, ABC, NBC, and CBS, are owned or controlled by members of these organizations.

Another leading Bilderberg is the Canadian, Conrad Black, the head of the Hollinger Group, which owns a stream of newspapers and magazines in Canada, the United States, Britain, Israel and elsewhere. These include the Jerusalem Post,

Telegraph newspapers in London, and 52% of newspapers in Canada.

All of these are owned, in truth, by British Intelligence, a key pillar of the Brotherhood and major suspect in the murder of Diana. During the last war, an elite wing of British Intelligence called the Special Operations Executive set up a front organization called War Supplies, Ltd. This was run by two SOE agents called George Montegu Black and Edward Plunket Taylor, a leading expert on economic warfare, who later wrote the banking laws of the Bahamas and the Cayman Islands.

After the war it continued under Taylor and Black as a front for British Intelligence and its name was changed to the Argus Corporation. Later it became the Hollinger Group headed by Bilderberger Conrad Black, the son of George Montagu Black, the British Intelligence Agent who set the whole thing up in the first place. It was also British Intelligence who created, and still controls, the CIA.

All this is going on all the time, and 99.999% of humanity, even those who consider themselves "informed," have no idea these organizations even exist, let alone what they are doing.

JR: If you take a large corporation like Bayer or Dow or any of these, and you begin to look at their subsidiaries around the world, the list goes on for pages and pages and pages and pages. Each subsidiary a small line on a page. This subsidiary is itself a large corporation in some country and it obviously plays a dominant role in that society, especially when you get to the Third World. There are no other big companies like this in the Third World.

How do you feel these fit in with the secret societies which we've talked about, and this global elite at the top of the agenda?

DI: In the end all roads lead to the same few people and this same few organizations that we've talked about. When you get to the top of the pyramid in the transnational corporation network, you are hitting the same people who control all these corporations. So as you quite rightly say, you take one corporation like Bayer, then you list all the subsidiaries it owns all over the world — but Bayer is in itself a subsidiary. This is the staggering thing. It is like a massive Christmas tree which goes eventually goes up to the elite, the "fairy," at the top.

The Robber Barons

David Icke (DI): Control of money is vital to the agenda. The wealth of the world has been sucked into the hands of the few via the world financial system. The same people who have controlled the politicians have controlled the banks over the years. Legislation has been passed which allows banks all over the world to lend at least 10 times what they have on deposit. It's far more than that in reality. So every time you put a dollar in the bank you are giving the bank the right to lend at least ten that it doesn't have.

People think, because that's what we are led to believe, that governments create money. No, no. The vast overwhelming majority of what we call "money" comes into circulation by private banks making loans called credit which are just figures on a screen. Such money doesn't exist.

If everyone went back to the bank tomorrow and wanted to take out what they theoretically have on deposit, the bankers would slam the door in 20 minutes because they haven't got it, they haven't even got a fraction of it. It's just a myth that we have that money in the bank. We don't. The bank doesn't have it.

Control over creation of the units of exchange, which we call money, have been handed to private banks owned by the same elite I've been talking about. The Federal Reserve, the so-called central bank of America, which is neither federal nor has any reserve, has control over United States interest rates. The level of interest rates affects how many people want loans. That affects how many units of exchange are in circulation, which affects whether we have a boom or a bust. We have given control of the entire system to the Brotherhood which, in fact, created the system in the first place.

Look at an economic boom, when there is prosperity, jobs, homes, when people have enough to eat. Look at an economic depression when a lot of people lose their homes, lose their jobs, don't have enough to eat. The only difference between those two states is the amount of units of exchange in circulation at the time. So what happens is that banks in the first stage of the scam make lots of loans and keep interest rates down. Lots of units of exchange are being put into circulation, lots of economic activity follows, people buy things, there are jobs, and families can pay the rent.

During a boom people and companies invariably get more in debt because they get confident. They say, hey, I have a lot of money in the bank but —

JR: Let's expand.

DI: — yes, let's expand. I'm going to have two holidays this year, I'm going to have a bigger car, got to have a bigger house. I haven't got the money but I can borrow it. Times are good. I can pay it back. More "money" in circulation means more economic activity, more demand for products, so companies borrow more "money" which doesn't exist to expand production.

That is, in effect, the fishing rod being thrown out by the banks. Then comes stage two as the fishing rod is reeled in. What the banks do is increase interest rates, so depressing the demand for loans. Fewer units of exchange are in circulation because fewer loans are being made. Economic activity starts to fall. When you have a depression, it is not because people have decided they don't want to eat or they don't want a job or they want to lose their home. It is because there are not enough units of exchange in circulation.

JR: This reminds me of a conversation I had with a researcher who told me that during the American depression of 1929, there were somewhere between 1,200 to 1,500 private currencies issued. People had gotten together and they had looked around and said, well, Washington may be broke and those dollars may be useless, but there's nothing wrong with us intrinsically. So they began to print their own money. This is a great chapter of untold history in America where people traded, bartered in a sense, but they used their own money and they survived by not hooking into that whole federal system.

DI: This is a very good point. This is about taking power back and not just accepting like a sheep the structure that you are told you must conform to. The final scene of this fishing line out, fishing line in, scam is that when people can no longer pay back their loans because of the manipulated depression they go bankrupt. When this happens the banks have the right to take possession of wealth that does exist, their customers' land, homes, and businesses.

In this way, the wealth of the world, the real wealth, has been sucked to the top of this pyramid and this is why so few hands now control the real wealth of the world. They've been playing this game — boom-bust, boom-bust — for centuries.

Third World debt, which is crucifying our fellow humanity, is debt on money that has never, does not, and will never exist, because when you take out a loan no one prints any money, no one mints any coins, no one moves any precious metal a single inch. All they do is type the amount of your loan on to a screen, and then you start paying interest on it. It's just figures on a screen. It's a massive confidence trick.

Governments could print their own money interest-free, put it into circulation interest-free instead of borrowing it from the private banking cartels and the taxpayers paying interest on it. They don't do that because the politicians are controlled by the Brotherhood which controls the banking system.

So you've got no major political party anywhere in the world that is actually suggesting that governments print their own money and stop paying interest on it to private banks. Incidentally, both John F. Kennedy and Abraham Lincoln were starting to introduce interest-free money in some small form and they both met the same fate, which I am sure was not pure coincidence. What we can do is start stepping out of the system. When I wrote a book in the late 1980s called It Doesn't Have to Be Like This,* I found in Britain two "LETS" (Local Exchange and Trading System) groups, systems of barter, in which people in effect created their own currency.

JR: There are many of those in the United States.

DI: Sure. Now they are all over Britain. This is why information about how the financial system really works is so important — so that people can de-link from it. Basically what happens during a depression is that people who need work and services are disconnected from people who have the skills to provide those services simply because there is no piece of paper (money) to exchange between the parties. So what we need to do in our communities is work out schemes by which one person's contribution to another person can be rewarded. You can do that if you get together with a determination to do it.

JR: There is a huge movement of this kind in Britain these days?

DI: It's growing all the time.

JR: What is the government response to this?

---

* Subtitled, Green Politics Explained (London: Green Print, 1990).

DI: They are trying to work out ways of taxing it, of course, because they have a real problem. The way this system works is that you get one person in the community who sets himself up as the person who administers the organization and you invent a currency.

Money is not the root of all evil actually; it's the means to overcome the limitations of barter so that you can reward contributions to society without having to do a like-for-like exchange which can get complicated. So the unit of exchange called money, exchanging an energy for contributions to society, is extremely positive. It's not an evil. Where the problem comes in is when you start having interest on money, because then purely by controlling the unit of exchange you can control the world and suck people's wealth into your hands — which is what's happened.

So you invent a currency.

Someone provides a list of the skills that everyone in the group has and then people say, right, I want my front room painted. Here's a painter on the list. Will you do it? Okay. Yes, done. Then you ring the central administrator and you say, right, so many units to this man, the painter. And you've agreed on the price beforehand. Now this painter can go to someone else in the group and get services for himself to that extent without making any more contributions to the group. Basically you're earning money by the work that you are doing for other people which allows you to have units of exchange to use in that group for work that you need doing.

This helps you to delink from the rigged financial system and provide your own method of exchanging contributions to each other. It's actually very simple and it works very well.

JR: I know a group in Ithaca, New York, which is founded by Paul Glover, and it works on that principle. They have their own newspaper now, in which they publish stories of people who have gotten into their network and have actually changed their lives. They've decided, well, I think I will do what I actually want to do instead of doing the thing that I thought I had to do to make that money over there. Now doing this instead I suddenly discover there are a few people, at least to begin with, who want what I do. Lo and behold, I can become part of an economic network. They have, at last count, 2000 individuals and business who have signed on, including a bank in Ithaca that is taking their money. They call the money "Ithaca Hours" paper. They claim it is less counterfeitable than American money.

So this guy sells his how-to kit to people for a very small amount and other people have started to introduce this currency too.

DI: It's a way of stepping out of the system. Meyer Amschel Rothschild, the man who founded the Rothschild empire, once said very memorably, "Give me control of a nation's currency and I care not who makes the laws." Control the currency and you control the country. And what we're talking about here is actually taking back control of the units of exchange. If we can't get control immediately of the units of exchange that are being used to manipulate us, then let's create our own and let's step out of this system as best we can.

This whole scam is held together merely because we take it seriously. It's our thought-energy that is holding it together. Someone pointed out something very true. If you pass a dollar across the counter in a shop you'll buy something. And the person who took your dollar will buy something else with it. People are taking that piece of paper seriously.

JR: Very seriously.

DI: Then someone points out, hey, hold on a minute, this is not legitimate, this dollar is counterfeit. Immediately the thought-form and the perception of that piece of paper is changed. Now it is worth nothing. It was buying things before when people were taking it seriously; now it's worthless. The piece of paper hasn't changed, only people's perception of it. Let's stop taking this system seriously and start walking away from it, not fighting it, not creating more conflict and frustration. Just say okay, you want to do that, I'm going to create my own system. I'm not going to fight you, I'm going to walk away from you and do something different that makes my life work. Then the energy, the thought-forms that are holding this system together are withdrawn and the whole thing collapses.

JR: This reminds me of the conversation we had the other day when we were talking about diversity being such an essential ideal.

DI: Absolutely vital.

JR: People live their own reality as opposed to only the consensus reality. There will then be so many realities it will be impossible to control them from a central point.

DI: If you look at what we've been talking about, it's been the desire by this Brotherhood to make everything uniform, uniform business, education, government, money, because they want one entity which they can then control, one uniform entity.

Living your own truth is the greatest form of rebellion. The more you express your uniqueness and live your own truth and live your own life in the way that you think is right, you are actually creating billions of different realities instead of the one the few can control. Suddenly, where do they start? "How do I manipulate this person because he's living this life and he's living that, how do I ..."

Suddenly you don't have one sheep herd consciousness to manipulate anymore. So we don't need smoke-filled rooms and new political parties. We don't need guns and all this stuff to meet the challenge of withdrawing from this control. We need billions of people to express their uniqueness, recognize their uniqueness, and live it and allow other people to live it. This whole edifice will come tumbling down because we are holding it together. Money is very, very vital to this because it is one of the great forms of control.

The Brotherhood of Knowledge

Jon Rappoport (JR): You believe that a type of knowledge possessed in Atlantis emerged into societies like Egypt or Sumeria. That it was grasped eventually by people like the Templars, and used to make them suddenly expand their operation, so that it could eventually control the destiny of Europe, or at least put them in serious competition with the Church.

Whether or not this knowledge was basically about practical matters, such as the supposed Masonic knowledge of engineering, or of organizational systems that could be applied to banking, or whether we are talking about something that goes much deeper in some spiritual sense, you are saying this knowledge was perverted, used as a medium of controlling other people. I would like to hear what you have to say about these things.

David Icke (DI): I think what we are seeing in the modern world is what happened at the end of Atlantis.

To understand the plot and the methods, we need to understand what consciousness and creation really are. Everything is energy, vibrating energy. We are all part of the same whole. We are like droplets of water in an ocean of consciousness. We are individual to an extent but we are all part of a whole.

We are everything that exists and we live forever because energy cannot be destroyed, only transmuted into another form. It has been vital for the Brotherhood agenda to persuade us to forget who we really are and identify ourselves as "ordinary," "powerless," and "insignificant." This way we operate at a fraction of our true powers and potential and become easy to herd and control.

One of the key ways this is done is get us to mistake what we are for what we are experiencing. Ask someone what they are and they will say "I am an American airline pilot," or "I am an English roadsweeper." That is not what we are. It is merely what we are experiencing on the eternal journey of evolution through experience. We are everything that exists having those experiences, we are not those experiences. When you see yourself as the Divine whole incarnate, your whole vision of life completely transforms. When you identify with your experiences, you see yourself in desperately limited terms. That's the idea.

Everything is "magnetic energy." Vibrational magnetism I call it. The nature of the magnetism is decided by thought, by thought fields, which make the energy vibrate at certain rates. If I sit here and I think thoughts of hate, then my thought patterns will resonate the energy around me to the frequency of that emotion. People near me will feel that. If I think thoughts of love then I generate that vibrational field around me. People will feel that too.

Our thoughts and emotions set the frequency of our energy field/consciousness and whatever our vibrational state, we will attract to us other energy fields (people, places, ways of life, experiences), which synchronize vibrationally with whatever we are giving out. We are like magnets attracting what we need to experience to face our inner selves and so evolve by understanding ourselves more deeply. Whatever our inner reality, this process re-creates it as an outer, physical, reality, in the people, places, experiences we attract.

Therefore if you think you are "ordinary," powerless, and insignificant, you will create an ordinary, powerless, and uneventful life experience. This is not because you are ordinary and powerless, merely because you think you are. The Brotherhood know this and they know that if they can condition your vision of yourself and the world, they will be manipulating your physical experience. That is serious knowledge when you have it and the vast majority of people do not.

Also, if you understand how this vibrational magnetism works, you can create fantastic technology that can do amazing things. You can make great chunks of rock weightless by enclosing them in a magnetic field which de-links them from gravity. This is how the ancients and the extraterrestrials built those vast structures we would struggle to build even today. Some flying saucers — one manifestation of them anyway — appear to use this same process. They are actually operating in their own universe vibrationally. Therefore it is, in effect, weightless compared with what it would be under the gravitational laws.

The knowledge being suppressed by the Brotherhood could transform the world. The knowledge used today to mind-control people is the same knowledge which could heal the mentally ill. There are microchips around today which can heal people with spinal injuries who would normally be in a wheelchair. Not just allow them to walk, but walk virtually like anyone else. That is being suppressed because they do not want the knowledge in the public arena. Instead, the microchip is being used as a form of tagging, a form of control, etc. This knowledge of vibrational fields can give us free and limitless energy with no pollution and stimulate abundant growth in the most inhospitable climate or terrain.

JR: You have no doubt that certain technologies are being kept out of public view? A number of technologies?

DI: Oh yes, I've met some of the scientists who have developed them, but do not make them public because of the threats to the lives of themselves and their families.

The Mind Doctors

Jon Rappoport (JR): What about mind-control technology?

David Icke (DI): There are references in ancient texts to what is called the "evil eye." It's become a cliché in the modern world for giving someone an unpleasant look. The evil eye, it seems to me, is a symbolic representation of what has become known in various parts of the world as voodoo and other names. This is the ability to fire malevolent thought fields into someone's aura, consciousness. By unbalancing a person's magnetic fields and planting highly negative thought fields you can cause physical, mental, and emotional illness. You can affect the way they think, you can make them go very strange in the head, become mentally ill, you can make them become physically ill.

JR: I and many other people have seen military and intelligence documents which indicate use or testing of chemicals and electronic devices for this purpose. Of course, there is a huge literature on formal and informal mind-control programs run by various governments.

DI: I have investigated what you might call the "satanic pyramid," the satanic rings of ritual abuse, child murder and ritual sacrifice, and the blood drinking ceremonies, all this staggering horror that is going on behind the facade of "normal" life.

As I have clawed my way up that pyramid, I have found the same names that I have identified in the manipulation of the banking pyramid, the political pyramid, and so on. It seems to me that above the people you can identify in the public domain — that I expose in "... and the truth shall set you free" — lie the most advanced black magicians on the planet, and ultimately the malevolent extraterrestrial group which controls them. They use their knowledge to keep those in the public domain in constant terror of them.

There are people lower down the various pyramids, the mass of the people who are in terror of losing their job, frightened of what people think of them, and so are conforming to what they believe other people think they should do. The further you go up the pyramid you enjoy more and more material reward, but the consequences for not doing exactly as demanded get more and more horrific. This "voodoo" knowledge, then, is used to manipulate the minds and health of people, and to control through fear even those working for you.

After one of my public talks, a lady came up to me. Her husband had died a year before. She was still quite young, she would be in her 30s, maybe. She said her husband had been a member of the American military's Psychic Assassination Squad. When people join the military, and we know this anyway, they are constantly assessing them and looking for signs that they have particular abilities that can be used for the furtherance of this control-agenda. For example, they are looking for people with powerful energy, particularly powerful thought projections and psychic abilities.

They get these people around the table and they give them a picture of someone they want to kill or manipulate. They might give them a possession, an object that resonates to the vibrational field of the target. It helps these psychics tune into the target's unique vibration. Then they do the American military version of voodoo.

They project thought fields at the person and they impregnate his aura with unbalanced malevolent vibrational fields which either affect him mentally, give him a mental breakdown, or affect him physically, causing a heart attack or cancer or whatever. Because, if you look at cancer, it is merely the cell-replacement mechanism of the body going out of balance and producing cells in an uncontrolled manner. If you can create an imbalance via this process of projecting thought fields, you stimulate cancer because whole cell-replacement systems go haywire. Human magnetic fields govern the replacement of cells so if you disrupt that you can cause mayhem. The Brotherhood has been doing this for thousands of years.

Look at this secret society that emerged in the Middle East — and I am sure it is still going today — called the Assassins. They were around the same time as the Templars. My research has shown that the Templars and the Assassins were working together, at least at the top of those organizations they were.

You have the Assassins who were supposed to have been the secret society on the side of the Muslims in the Crusades working together with the Templars who were supposed to be working for the Christian side in the Crusades. Anyone who has done research into how the modern world is manipulated will certainly recognize that little scam of operating through both "sides" at the same time.

One meaning of the word "Assassin" is "User of Hashish." The Assassins used drugs to create mind-controlled killers to murder the leaders of their enemies. Hence we get the word assassin in modern usage. Eventually they took out enough people so that those in positions of power realized that if they did not do what the Assassins said, they were going to get murdered. Just the threat was enough to ensure compliance. So it is today.

If you can hoard the esoteric knowledge for yourself and keep the public in ignorance of it, you can affect events and people in ways the public does not even believe are possible. You also stop the endless positive uses of this knowledge. It is no accident for me that we are talking about esoteric knowledge which has been dismissed in the public domain as devil-inspired or lunacy. When you talk about some of this stuff people say, "Oh you're mad mate, you're mad." Or, "You're the devil, it's the occult." These responses have been conditioned and encouraged, and they keep the flow of this secret knowledge out of the public domain, and in the hands of the Brotherhood who uses it against us.

JR: That makes quite a fantastic backdrop for talking about what is going on with some of the mind-control episodes we are hearing about, whether they come out of the organized MK-Ultra project of the CIA or the later Office of Research and Development at the CIA, or whether they are something less visible than even that. People want to know how far-flung this is, what the agenda is and how it is operating in our society.

Two years ago I located public testimony given before a Presidential Commission in Washington in March of 1995 by three women, a therapist and two of her patients, who claimed that they had been part of U.S. government radiation experiments. They said they had received radiation, but it was part of a wider mind-control program.

They gave that testimony and there was quite a response apparently at the time but absolutely no mainstream press ever covered it. So, like you, people have come to me over the years with stories about this. Different versions, different groups, different situations, different locations under the auspices of government agencies, of corporations, myriad stories about this sort of thing occurring. I would just like to get your take on that.

DI: First of all, that is all true, and if people understandably find it hard to believe, they need to appreciate the mentality which controls the United States and the other countries of the "free" world.

Let me give you the example of the Skull and Bones Society. One of the flags the Templars flew on their ships was the skull and bones. They used skulls in their rituals. That was pointed out when they were purged in France. In the comic books, of course, the skull and bones flag has become the flag of the pirate ship. Some esotericists say there are positive ceremonies involving skulls used symbolically. I can't get my head round that one, if you'll pardon the pun.

This has yet more significance to America. One of the most infamous, perhaps the most infamous, secret society in America is based at Yale University and it is called the Skull and Bones Society. It is called the Skull and Bones because it is another mask on the same face that relates back to the Templars and beyond — the same Brotherhood stream in which they do their blood drinking ceremonies and their skull worship.

The most famous Skull and Bones member today is George Bush. His father Prescott Bush was also a member. Prescott funded Hitler through the Harriman organization as I document in "... and the truth shall set you free." Skull and Bones initiates invariably end up in positions of overt or covert power. So it was with George Bush. He was born into the Brotherhood. He was groomed from the start to become head of the CIA, head of the Republican Party at the time of the Watergate Hearings, Vice President and then President of the United States.

These are the guys, the blood drinking Satanists, who are running the world. The mental, emotional, and physical abuse of people — including children — is part of their way of life.

The more that I have looked at what is going on in the world, the more obvious it is that in the end we are looking at the mind and the emotions as the key both to how we got into this mess and how we get free of it. The only way a few people can control the masses is by manipulating their minds and emotions to see the world as they want them to see it. That, for want of a term, is the battleground on which this whole drama is being played out — the human mind and the human emotions.

It is interesting when you look at my definition of mind control: it is to manipulate someone's mind so they think, and therefore behave, the way you want them to. Under that definition of mind control, the question is not how many people on the planet are mind controlled, it is how many are not. The answer is hardly any.

JR: When you look at what happens in all these mind-control projects, are the objectives the same?

DI: If you take these notorious mind-control projects like MK-Ultra, run by the CIA and other agencies, what are they doing? They are seeking to wipe people clean of a sense of uniqueness, their sense of self, their sense of who they are, their sense of independent thinking, of filtering, of questioning, and to replace that with a personality that simply reacts as desired to whatever stimuli are imposed or whatever order or trigger is given. They create robots.

Then take it to the next level, and look at what they do to people when they join the military. From day one all over the world, they are seeking to wipe those people clean of their sense of uniqueness, their sense of self, their sense of who they are, their sense of questioning, of filtering information and thinking for themselves. They want to create robotic hired killers. So some bloke in a peak cap shouts an order and a group of guys start shooting at brown-faced people or others who have never done them any bloody harm. They would probably have a beer with them in the bar if they were allowed to get to know them. But they shoot because they are robots.

I think it is important we stop beating about the bush. When you join the military you are agreeing to become a robot. You are handing over your mind with your civilian suit. I know there has been a lot of controversy in America about whether gays should be allowed to join the military. I have a very simple philosophy on this. Anyone dumb enough to want to join the military ought to be allowed to do so. In short, they want to take away uniqueness and replace it with a "yes, sir" personality.

Then we come to the mass of the people and exactly the same thing is happening. They want people to give up their right to think, their uniqueness, and replace that with a personality which reacts to certain stimuli. This is why Problem-Reaction-Solution works every time. People don't think or question. They see the veil and miss what is behind it.

It is worth considering the background to the

mind-control projects like MK Ultra. The two World Wars were created by the Brotherhood and they played the different "sides" off against each other to create a conflict which led to the United Nations, the European Union, and much centralization of global power. An offshoot of this were the mind-control projects that we have today.

Back in the early part of this century there was a secret society called the Round Table which was set up in London, which is the epicenter of the Brotherhood. Germany and France too, but London and the British Isles particularly. The front man of the Round Table was a guy called Cecil Rhodes after whom Rhodesia was named. He openly called for world government.

The elite members of the Round Table from America, like Edward Mandel House and Bernard Baruch, were the major players in the American war cabinet in the First World War. The elite members of the Round Table from Britain, like the Rothschild-controlled banker, Alfred Milner, were the key players in the British war administration in the First World War. They orchestrated the First World War. At the Versailles Peace Conference, near Paris, in 1919 they met again and the same people who created the war were appointed by their various countries to decide how the world would be shared out and redrawn as the result of the war! Problem-Reaction-Solution.

You had the same in the Second World War, where precisely the same thing happened. In "... and the truth shall set you free," I show how both the sinking of the Lusitania and the attack on Pearl Harbor were created by the Brotherhood to manipulate the United States into the wars, and both presidents, Wilson and Roosevelt, knew exactly what was going on. Hitler was funded from Britain and America, not least by the Rockefellers' Standard Oil. Hitler's notorious chemical conglomerate, I. G. Farben, which operated the labor camp at Auschwitz, was, in effect, the same company as Standard Oil.

The Brotherhood funded and supported the Nazis and the "Allies" who "opposed" them. The idea was to create a war which changed the world dramatically, and that's what happened. Out of the Second World War came the mind-control projects we have today. Near the end of the War, all sides wanted to make sure the knowledge of mind control gleaned from the experiments in the concentration camps would not be lost by having Nazi scientists sentenced to death by the Nuremberg Trials.

So British Intelligence and American Intelligence launched Project Paperclip. Its aim was to get out of Nazi Germany the key mind-control experimenters and the genetic manipulators. Josef Mengele was among them. Some went to South America, some went to the United States. I'm sure some went to Britain also to continue their work. These were the Nazis who inspired MK-Ultra in the years that followed and other mind-control projects. MK-Ultra had 149 offshoots alone.

The Nazis were becoming experts in something

called Trauma Based Mind Control. There is a mechanism in the mind which shuts out memories of severe trauma. People often cannot remember road accidents, really bad ones, because the mind has compartmentalized those memories and closed them off from the rest of their mind.

This is a good thing because people do not want to keep reliving some of the horrors that happen to them on the highway. But the Nazis realized this could be used to control people. In the concentration camps they had an endless stream of prisoners on whom to experiment and they found that if you systematically traumatize people, particularly if you get them before the age of five or six, you can turn their minds into a honeycomb of self-contained compartments, none of which are aware of the others' existence.

In the aftermath of the Second World War, when these Nazi scientists continued their work in other parts of the world, mind-control projects started to appear. These projects are using children in increasingly vast numbers. They are inflicting upon them from a very early age, from birth where possible, horrendous sexual abuse, violence, and ritual torture. They make them watch babies being sacrificed, and make them drink blood. They even make them sacrifice children themselves. They are sexually abused, some of them by top politicians. I have met people who have survived some of these projects. I list a stream of famous names in I Am Me, I Am Free (Bridge of Love, 1996.)

What this does is create within these children

something that has become known as Multiple Personality Disorder or DID, Dissociative Identity Disorder. Their minds break up into a series of compartments which are isolating and shutting out memories of trauma. The mind doctors also use techniques to create hypnotic "walls" to imprison those memories, particularly when they involve top politicians or famous people. They also install "suicide triggers," so if that part of the mind is ever accessed, the suicide triggers are activated and people kill themselves. Many people who in more recent times have started to remember what happened to them have committed suicide, or tried to, for this reason.

Therapists have been working with these people by trial and error, because the knowledge of how the mind control and the triggers are imposed are naturally top secret. But the therapists are getting more street-wise now and they are overcoming the suicide triggers more and more. Increasing numbers of people, particularly after the age of 30, are beginning to remember what happened to them and who did it. The compartments are breaking down. The common themes in their account of names, agendas, organizations, methods, and rituals are very obvious. Many recall their experiences in great detail.

Of course there has been a quickly organized response to try to discredit this emerging information. The strategy is to blame it on the therapists who are "putting this knowledge into people's minds."

One organization, set up in a number of countries to discredit the people who are remembering their abuse, is called the False Memory Syndrome Foundation. It's very enlightening to look at some of the principal players in this organization. On the advisory board of the American False Memory Syndrome Foundation is a notorious CIA mind-controller and robot-creator from the University of California [Los Angeles] called Louis West. Also on the same board alongside him is a guy called Dr. Martin Orne, from the University of Pennsylvania, another mind manipulator involved in MK-Ultra.

And you will also find another guy called James Randi, who is a so-called magician who has been wheeled onto television a number of times in Britain, to discredit any accounts of the "paranormal," and to ridicule people who are having psychic experiences. James Randi is on the board of the False Memory Syndrome Foundation, which is trying to discredit recovered memories of ritual abuse and pedophile activity against children.

I would stress that we are not dealing with coincidence here. When Patty Hearst came out of the Symbionese Liberation Army, she was given a "mental examination" by Louis West, the notorious mind manipulator. When Timothy McVeigh was in captivity before his trial for the Oklahoma City bombing he was given a "mental examination" by Louis West — which will explain a lot of what followed, I am sure. So these are mind-controllers who are fronting up an organization whose purpose is to discredit the people who have been mind controlled!

But what these mind manipulators have misunderstood is the power of the human spirit. What they thought were programmed people for life are now starting to remember. It is a massive Achilles heel that I do not think they bargained for because there are so many people now starting to speak out. The mind-controllers are going to run out of digits to stick in the dike and they are going to face the tidal wave in the next few years.

The Mind-Controlled Assassins

David Icke (DI): So why are people mind controlled? Some are used to assassinate people. How many times do we hear "lone nut, no conspiracy" when a famous person is murdered? People are programmed to become obsessed with the famous person and then they kill him or her. Of course the public says, "Oh yeah, he was never a full picnic. He was always a bit strange. He was always obsessed with so and so." No one asks why he was strange and who made him strange. It is written off as an unfortunate thing that happens in the world. The guy got shot by a nut.

Look at Sirhan Sirhan, the guy who was convicted of killing Bobby Kennedy. Sirhan had just been on a "mind expansion" course when he started writing things in his diary like: "Kill Kennedy." His psychiatric report shows that this guy was in a mind-controlled state. There was a woman he talks about meeting in the Ambassador Hotel where Kennedy was shot. She was never found. It is very clear to me looking at the evidence that she gave him a trigger. It can be a word, a sentence, a sign, a sound, it can be almost anything. Whatever they choose to program into a compartment [in the mind] to activate the subconscious instructions. Suddenly you start following the programming: "Kill Kennedy." There is some doubt that Sirhan's gun killed Bobby Kennedy, but that's not the point. He's there with a gun, and so you can charge him with a murder carried out by someone else.

These things are used all the time to take people out. In the British mind programs, they call those who are very powerfully mind controlled "Dead Eyes." One of the most famous "Dead Eyes" was a guy called Thomas Hamilton. He was the man who went into a gymnasium in a school in Dunblane in Scotland and blew away a lot of little children. He was programmed. I know from therapists I have spoken to that he was a Dead Eye. It is the same with a guy called Martin Bryant who went crazy with a gun in the street in a place called Port Arthur in Tasmania not long after Dunblane. We see people again and again all over the world who "go crazy" with guns who are written off as nuts. Many of them commit suicide, so destroying the evidence. Thomas Hamilton did that. It is part of their programming to kill the evidence.

The mass consciousness is also being subjected to trauma-based mind control. Think about Dunblane and Port Arthur. The control-agenda is to take guns out of circulation among the general population. I speak as someone who would not pull a trigger to save my life. I do not see the point. I would rather leave this world in peace than add to the violence. But lots of people would rather keep the guns for self-protection, and the Brotherhood wants to disarm them while further arming their agencies of control, the police, the FBI, and the military.

It is obviously easier to take over an unarmed population. So there is undoubtedly a campaign, globally, coming from this same Brotherhood, to take weapons out of circulation. If you look at the effect of these guys who go crazy with guns, it is classic Problem-Reaction-Solution. After a mass shooting at Hungerford in England, a lot of weapons were taken out of circulation. In the wake of Thomas Hamilton and Dunblane, even more have been confiscated and certain weapons have been banned. Purely as a result of what Martin Bryant did in Port Arthur, Tasmania, laws have been passed to take weapons out of circulation on a massive scale in Australia. So it goes on around the world.

But there are other reasons for these horrific mass killings. I remember driving down a motorway (what Americans call a freeway) and stopping at a gas station, a petrol station. I had been working the previous day and I had not heard the news. I looked at the newspapers on the stand and I saw this picture of a class of little kids. I read the headline and I read the first three paragraphs. It was the news about Dunblane and I felt traumatized. I felt it so deeply. Just for a few seconds I went numb.

What that event did was traumatize the collective mind of Britain and much further afield. As above, so below. As with the individual consciousness, so with the collective. As is well known, a traumatized mind is far more open to manipulation and suggestion. Of course, what is coming through the television and advertising is hypnotic suggestion. They are talking to our subconscious most of the time because again they understand how to feed subliminal messages via certain phrases and symbols.

Breaking the Spirit

Jon Rappoport (JR): When I was writing about the Oklahoma City bombing,* it became quite clear to me that demoralization is one of the main "benefits" that accrues to the powers-that-be. A general futility sets in in the population alongside their fear. The active spirit for change, for challenging the status quo, is punctured like a balloon. More passivity becomes the order of the day. The authorities are elevated. The public in effect says, "You take care of this. Do whatever you have to. Strip away the Bill of Rights. Just get these maniacs out of our world."

The psychology of this is so obvious. In the wake of that kind of demoralization, people lower their sights, their expectations about life. They will take less and be happy with it because their new view of life is that it is less. They'll accept less freedom, less power, less understanding. They'll surrender their will and think they're doing the right thing.

David Icke (DI): The elite want the people all over the world to be in fear and to not feel safe.

---

* Jon Rappoport, Oklahoma City Bombing: The Suppressed Truth (Escondido, CA: The Book Tree, 1997).

Whenever anyone is in fear of anything they give their power away to anyone they think can protect them from what they have been manipulated to fear. I think it was the Daily Mail in London, one of the major tabloids in Britain, which ran a front-page headline after the Port Arthur shooting by Martin Bryant. It said, "IS NOWHERE IN THE WORLD SAFE ANYMORE?" That is the reaction the Brotherhood is seeking. They choose their locations with this in mind. Thomas Hamilton went into a school in a little place called Dunblane where everyone felt safe. He did not do it in downtown gangland Glasgow. The town of Hungerford is the same. Martin Bryant didn't open fire in the downtown drug areas of Sydney. He did it in a quiet little community in Tasmania where everyone felt safe. The Brotherhood are looking for this reaction: "Well, if it could happen there, it could happen to me, oh my God!" Make them feel fearful and insecure. Make them give their power away, and demand power to the police to protect them from what they are manipulated to fear.

So these things are happening multidimensionally all the time. None of these events happens for one reason. They happen for many reasons because they know that events like that have multidimensional effects on people.

Ritual Child Abuse

David Icke (DI): These mind-controlled slaves and children are also forced to meet the sexual desires of very famous people, entertainers as well as businessmen and politicians. These kids are used to compromise others in politics and business, etc., whom the Brotherhood want under their control.

They look for the person's weakness. Does he have a weakness for money? Okay, we'll bring him a load of money and he will do what we want. If he is not into that, does he have a weakness for position and status in society? Okay, we will give him a title or we will make him ambassador to this, or whatever.

What they do in Britain is they make them a Lord or a Sir, they do it that way. "I am sure the Queen will recognize your contribution when the next Queen's honors list comes round if you just happen to do this to serve your country." All that stuff. If none of that works, do they have a weakness sexually, and often, do they have a weakness for children sexually?

I have talked to an increasing number of people both in Britain and in America who have been sexually abused from a very early age and put through satanic ritual abuse by very famous people.

Actually not long before we are talking here, I went up to a place called Bohemian Grove in northern California in among the Redwood trees and in a very closely guarded area. The global elite from all over the world meet to go through very strange ceremonies at least once a year. I have been talking to some of the people who have been in these government mind-control projects. They've been used for some horrific torture and ritual sacrifice ceremonies at the Bohemian Grove. You see why most of those in these mind-control projects don't live to tell the tale.

Look at the work of John DeCamp, a State Senator in Nebraska, who started investigating a savings and loan financial scandal involving the Franklin Credit Union. This revolved around a Republican big-wig called Lawrence King who sang the National Anthem at the Republican Convention in 1984 and 1988. He went to jail for embezzling something like 40 million dollars from the Franklin Credit Union.

As a result of his research, DeCamp wrote a book called the Franklin Cover-up: Child Abuse, Satanism and Murder in Nebraska,* because he met people who were talking about the pedophile rings that Lawrence King operated. One of the guests at King's pedophile parties was George Bush, the close friend of Queen Elizabeth II and Prince Philip. I have heard this from a couple of sources.

---

* Revised edition (Lincoln, NE: AWT, Inc., 1995).

Then there is Operation Brownstone which was operated from a building in Virginia not far from Washington D.C. during the Bush administration. Children were supplied for Congressmen and other people they wanted to compromise. Hidden cameras were in the rooms. Top businessmen as well as politicians were involved.* When a video of their sexual activities is produced, it is amazing how these people do exactly what the Brotherhood wants them to do.

JR: Why the blood drinking? Is it just perversion or is there more to it?

DI: The Chinese have an ancient healing system which they call acupuncture. This is based on the network of energy lines and vortexes, or "chakras" which interpenetrate the physical and spiritual bodies. These relate to the network of magnetic lines of energy that go around the Earth.

These energy lines carry the lifeforce; their physical expression are the arteries and the blood. The blood carries the lifeforce. The Brotherhood are obsessed with bloodlines and preserving bloodlines because way back in the ancient world they originate, I am sure, with an extraterrestrial race. The

---

* See Washington Times articles: "HOMOSEXUAL PROSTITU-TION PROBE ENSNARES OFFICIALS OF BUSH, REAGAN: 'CALL BOYS' TOOK MIDNIGHT TOUR OF WHITE HOUSE," June 29, 1989, A1, A7; "POWER BROKER SERVED DRUGS, SEX AT PARTIES BUGGED FOR BLACKMAIL" and "RNC CALLS SCANDAL A 'TRAGIC SITUA-TION,' June 30, 1989, A1, A7; "TOP JAPANESE POLITICIAN LINKED TO SPENCE," July 5, 1989, A1, A8; "U.S. EXPANDS PROBE OF 'CALL BOY' RING," July 6, 1989, A1, A10.

elite believe that certain bloodlines carry particularly powerful energy, psychic powers and other powers from this lifeforce in the blood. The Nazis called this the "Vril" power. I think some of this relates to the copper content.

When they have their blood rituals and their blood drinking ceremonies they believe they are absorbing energy, the lifeforce, and increasing their power. Their sexual rituals are linked with the blood rituals. Sexual energy is the creative force, a fantastic source of creative power. This is why, right through the centuries, the Brotherhood has used its Roman Church, and others, to pervert and suppress this energy. They have used fear and guilt to do this. If they can imbalance or suppress the flow of sexual energy, they are suppressing the flow and power of creative energy.

The other thing that I saw, and this is deeply unpleasant, is that in these cult rituals, sex with children — whether they were boys or girls — was overwhelmingly done through anal intercourse. So I thought, why is this? There has to be a reason. Then I met a therapist in London called Vera Diamond whom I have been working with. She has been helping to heal the minds of ritually abused and mind-controlled people for fifteen years.

She said the anal intercourse relates to something called vaso-vagal shock. When they have anal intercourse with a child, it is so painful that it sends a charge of energy, electricity, up the spine which explodes into the brain and it helps to split the mind into compartments — exactly what they want, of course.

She showed me paintings by some of her clients depicting how this felt. One was a self-portrait with a line of white energy streaming up the spine and exploding in the head. So again, nothing happens for one reason. These ritual satanic ceremonies are all part of a bigger picture. The word is: control.

There is another element in this and that's the destruction of innocence and purity. They want to destroy purity and they want to destroy innocence.

The stories these victims tell, which correspond in amazing detail, are absolutely horrific. It does, however, give you an idea of how it is possible to be so imbalanced that you can sit around a table and decide how to play countries off against each other in wars that produce 55 million casualties.

JR: It sounds as if you're saying there is an elite to whom war is actually a blood ritual. Is that what you're saying? That in some perverted way war is a spiritual experience to these manipulators?

DI: Yes. Absolutely. Not only do the alarm bells ring when you realize that Diana's car crashed on an ancient pagan sacrificial site, you start to realize why the Rockefellers gave land free of charge in New York for the United Nations building. This land was previously used as a slaughter house! The sacrifice, in effect, of animals. That is the land, that is the energy, on which the "building of peace" is actually built. Animal sacrifice is something else the manipulators are very much into in their rituals — when they are not killing people.

The Big Picture

Jon Rappoport (JR): How do you see the reaction of this elite to the blood ritual called war? Are they somehow psychically plugging themselves in to absorb the energy that is thrown off by all that blood? Is that what they are consciously trying to do?

David Icke (DI): Those are very good questions. I think we are getting into the bigger picture of all this now. If you do not take this into other dimensions, I think eventually you lose the plot. These people may be imbalanced, but are not stupid. They believe they are interacting with some kind of other consciousness. And they are.

We are multidimensional consciousness operating in many dimensions, all sharing the same space. It is similar to radio and television frequencies. Get a radio and you tune it to one of those frequencies and you lock into a station. In our physical embodiment now, we are tuned to this dense physical "station." We look out of our eyes and we are seeing this station, the physical world. But when you tune to one radio station it doesn't mean the others have disappeared. They are still broadcasting. It is only that we are not tuned to them. Move the dial from one frequency to another one and you pick up another station. We can do this with our minds. All these different frequencies and dimensions of life are sharing the same space.

We are all one gigantic consciousness experiencing in different ways. There is a level of us on every dimension. The question is: At any one time are we accessing a tiny fraction of all that exists, the higher dimensions and levels of consciousness open to us, or are we expanding our consciousness to access more and more of this infinite mind? The way we see ourselves and the world will be dramatically different, depending on which we choose. If the level of consciousness we are accessing is limited, our vision, perception and creative potential will also be limited.

It seems to me, the more I research this, that there is a dimension not far from this one which resonates to the frequency of low vibrational emotion: fear, guilt, resentment, and so on. Every time we are manipulated to feel fear, resentment, and guilt, we are, through our thoughts, creating energy fields which resonate to that frequency of low vibration emotion. We are feeding it, adding to its powers. In that sense a war becomes a vibrational banquet to this other frequency range. A level of us exists on that frequency range also. And I think it has become such a cesspool that it is acting as a vibrational prison, closing off the connection for most people to the higher dimensions. This is reflecting in the physical world as a physical prison, our sense of limitation and "I can't."

Some people have called this cesspool a negative force, some call it Satan, some call it Set. Every culture has its own name for it.

What I am talking about is not some guy with a tail and horns and a pitchfork, I am talking about a level of consciousness. These thought fields take on a life of their own. They become a collective consciousness of very low vibrational energy.

The satanic rituals, which are absolutely rampant all over the world, are interacting with this energy field, this frequency range, the cesspool vibration. There are entities, aspects of consciousness within that frequency, which I believe are possessing, in effect, the upper levels of the pyramid of the power elite on Earth.

It is interesting when you look at the initiation ceremonies in Brotherhood branches, like Skull and Bones Society. They are so malevolent, so unpleasant, they are creating a low vibrational field which allows possession to take place. They are tuning the consciousness of the initiate in to the frequency that I am talking about. It is certainly possible for entities from this cesspool frequency to manifest themselves physically so we can see them. I know people who have touched entities from other dimensions. It is like touching a real person who then simply disappears. They return to their own frequency.

This starts to explain the stories about "ghosts" and "extraterrestrials" all the way back into the ancient world. The descriptions correlate, also, with the way people have described "demons." It is amazing how many religions have begun because their founder claimed to have had a "vision" of some entity who manifested before him. Mohammed and Islam, Joseph Smith and the Mormons, are just two examples.

And how many "visions" of "Jesus" and the "Virgin Mary" have we had? When you have a "vision" that relates to the Bible, they build a shrine to you. When you see an entity not related to the Bible, they say you are communicating with the Devil!

To manifest physically from another dimension requires tremendous amounts of energy. This is why so many of these "visions" and manifestations happen near or on big Earth energy vortex points. Another way this can be done is by creating tremendous amounts of energy through the release of sexual energy, blood, etc. Then these entities can manifest in this dimension for a time.

I have heard many stories by people who seem very grounded to me, who say they were visited by strange entities. When they looked to watch them leaving, they had disappeared.

There is one guy who runs a garage in the middle of nowhere. Men arrived dressed in black, the classic Men in Black of UFO folklore. They didn't have a car, they just arrived. The garage owner was frightened and he felt an aura of evil around them. When he turned to see them walking away, they were not there. They could not have disappeared in any other way except out of this dimension.

Look at the Old Testament and some of the angry judgmental gods, and you can see this entity-manifestation happening. I think we have a vibrational prison around the planet consisting of low vibrational emotion and we are helping add to this every time we produce those emotions. Imagine how much of this a war can create.

When you start on the spiritual journey, when you open your mind and your heart to other possibilities, all hell often breaks loose in your life. Your life starts to fall apart. There is a good reason for this.

As we walk the spiritual path, we attract to us the people and experiences which will bring to the surface all of that low vibrational emotion we have not wanted to deal with. All the guilt, fear, and anger we have suppressed deep within ourselves. We have to face these suppressed emotions and heal them, transform them, because the journey to multi-dimensional wholeness is only possible when that level of us which resonates to the cesspool vibration is cleansed.

When we go through great emotional upheavals and challenges, we are taking down the prison walls within us which are disconnecting us from our higher dimensions of self. You could see our higher self as our mission control, giving us the bigger perspective and allowing us to observe information and events in the physical world from a higher, spiritual understanding. When we lose our powerful connection with our mission control we lose the bigger perspective and we are, for example, at the mercy of the media-information pouring in through the eyes and the ears — the very "information" controlled by the Brotherhood.

So what the power-elite want to do, and what they have largely been doing up to now, is isolate us from our higher mission control.

New Age Naiveté

Jon Rappoport **(JR):** What can people do to change this?

David Icke (DI): We change ourselves and we change the world because we are the world and the world is us. We are all the same energy and if we change ourselves we are changing the collective. This is happening, let no one despair. In every country I visit, it is happening.

When anyone starts to walk the road to spiritual freedom and open themselves to the higher dimensions of self, they become channels through which those higher energies can be projected into this physical dimension. We become like broadcasting transmitters for this energy and so we affect everyone around us to a larger or lesser extent. The more people do this, the quicker the world will transform into the paradise it could — and will — be. Many people who call themselves "New Age" are making a considerable contribution to this, but like everything it has its down side which we need to be aware of.

A lot of what is called "New Age" is not, in my experience, connecting with the higher levels of understanding. Open psyches which do not tune to these higher levels instead connect with some of the lower dimensions, including the Cesspool Vibration, and they can be seriously manipulated. There is a great deal of this going on, I feel.

To make the change most powerful and effective, we need to balance the male with the female, the spiritual with the physical, the right brain of intuition with the left brain of physical reality. While the physical is dominating the spiritual for most people, so much of the New Age is imbalanced in the other direction and it needs to get off the ceiling if it is going to make an effective contribution. Surely, we do not come into incarnation as physical entities to then seek to ignore that we have done so. We are here to transform the physical world, not escape from it.

One of the mind-controlled slaves I've met, who was attached to Henry Kissinger for many years, told me Kissinger was in right at the start of the creation of the New Age Movement. He was orchestrating it. He was putting people into the public arena to prime it and get it going.

They knew that a vibrational change was coming which would open the psyche of vast numbers of people to awaken from their mental slumber. What they needed to do was hijack this awakening and direct it into new prisons designed to entrap people. The New Age movement is their creation to a significant extent.

I see all this channeling that is going on. I hear about Ashtar Command, and Maitreya, and the Great White Brotherhood, and goodness knows who else isn't coming through. I think that originates within the cesspool vibration, or directly from the Brotherhood's "psychic transmissions," and I think it is massively manipulating. There are very, very few people who have genuinely gone through the transformation and emotional cleansing necessary to access real enlightenment on the higher dimensions and bring that down through the vibrations to the Earth plane. Some can do that, but much of it, I feel, is crap dressed up as inspiration.

I did read a book called Ashtar Command and the New World Order. It was apparently channeled by some unnamed New York businessman. Ashtar, an "extraterrestrial," who is representing the planetary alliance or something, says that world government, a world bank, and a world army is the way to bring oneness to the world. I thought, ah-hah, here we go. I think we need to be very streetwise and extremely wary of this whole New Age business. I have tremendous sympathy with its metaphysical basis and many of the concepts and the genuineness of many people involved with it, but it has become so ungrounded. It is a manipulator's orgasmic experience.

It is naiveté manifesting as spiritual enlightenment. I feel it needs to get off the ceiling and stop using spirituality as a form of escapism. We need to appreciate that anything, literally anything, can be manipulated to advance the Brotherhood agenda if people go round with their psyches open, but their eyes closed. I've heard people say that the communicator they are channeling is talking about love and so he must be genuine. But as with all manipulation, you need to tell people what they want to hear to pull people in. Then you twist the information and mislead them. If the channeler has a following, you mislead the followers too. I call it gin and tonic with a twist.

JR: What you're saying about the New Age reminds me of some of the UFO talk that's around.

DI: I think exactly the same applies in UFO research. It can be very misleading if people specialize in one area without lifting their heads and seeing how their subject connects with other areas of research. You get a very slanted, imbalanced view of what is going on. I think also if people are looking for one answer to everything they will wait forever. The truth is rarely black and white. It is a shade of gray. Finding the shade of gray, that's the trick. I think there are many reasons for the UFO phenomenon. I am not saying extraterrestrials do not exist. I am certainly not saying that. I think an extraterrestrial race has been behind the Brotherhood from the start and still is. However, I think this whole subject is being massively manipulated to advance the agenda.

I have no doubt that the elite in secret research projects in underground bases have what we call flying saucer technology. This presents tremendous potential for creating fear and Problem-Reaction-Solution scenarios. On Halloween night (no accident!), 1938, in Orson Welles' presentation of War of the Worlds, in a radio studio with special effects and actors, broadcasting, he said, "live" from the scene of a Martian landing. People panicked and there were traffic jams as people tried to escape the area where the "Martians" were supposed to be. This was with special effects and actors on a radio program. Could you imagine the possibilities if they flew large numbers of "space craft" over New York? I feel we are looking at a Problem-Reaction-Solution agenda unfolding here.

Look at the films that are coming out of Hollywood, stories based on fear of extraterrestrials. The X-Files as well. It is fear-based. Independence Day was an attack from unpleasant aliens. Perhaps we are leading up to some kind of announcement where the President of the day says there has not been a cover-up of knowledge and information about extraterrestrial activities around the planet but there has been a holding back of information, because they did not want to cause global panic. Now, the President might say, the situation has become so grave that he must report to the people of the world that there is a threat of an extraterrestrial invasion from a source unknown. I can see the President saying something like this:

> I call upon the people and the governments of the world and the leaders of the world to come together as one, to drop our individual differences among each other and focus on a common enemy, a common threat. I call upon the governments of the world to pool their military resources, their political resources and their administrative resources so that we can work as one unit to meet this common threat to mankind.

In other words, form a world army and a world

government.

Someone gave me a quote which is reported to have been said by Henry Kissinger at one of the secret meetings of the Brotherhood branch known as the Bilderberg Group. It apparently came out via a Swiss delegate. I don't know for certain if it's true but it perfectly fits the elite strategy for planetary control. Kissinger apparently said:

> Today Americans would be outraged if UN troops entered Los Angeles to restore order. Tomorrow they will be grateful. This is especially true if they were told there was an outside threat from beyond, whether real or promulgated, that threatened our very existence. It is then that all peoples of the world will plead with world leaders to deliver them from this evil. The one thing every man fears is the unknown. When presented with this scenario, individual rights will be willingly relinquished for the guarantee of well-being granted by their world government.

Two Sides
of the Same Face

Jon Rappoport (JR): When you write about groups who forward a planetary-control agenda, I think it's important that you be neither left nor right politically. So many researchers start with the premise that evil will be found in the camp of their ideological opposites. Christians call the United Nations satanic. Activists on the left are prone to labeling the bad guys capitalists. Arguments ensue. Accusations are made but nothing is settled. It turns out, for example, that the Trilateral Commission really does seek the compression of global power into the hands of a few.

But to say the Commission is the arm of the anti-Christ immediately pushes people on the political left to imagine that the Trilateralists may be good. Maybe they're really after international cooperation, unity, and so on. The whole dialogue, such as it is, degenerates into something pathetic. People end up saying that Gandhi was a racist because he met with the British, because he talked with them.

Believe me, there are nut-cases like this around today. I've seen them try to manipulate soft minds with the most polarizing accusations. For example, we now have a whole new generation of Americans who actually have faith in the Democratic Party because rabid racists have taken to trashing Bill Clinton.

David Icke (DI): This is an old trick. Get your enemy's enemy to attack you and suddenly your enemy sees you as the good guy. The Brotherhood works through all sides. We need to appreciate that this is not about right against left, or Christian against Jew. The Brotherhood can be found within all these organizations. The environmental movement is full of genuine people, but it is being used to advance the agenda.

In 1972, the Club of Rome produced a report called Limits to Growth which pump-primed the environmental movement. The Club of Rome is a Brotherhood front. I am not saying there is not an environmental problem. I was in what became known as the Green Movement during the 1980s for a time and was a national spokesman for a short while for the British Green Party. But I would ask the environmental movement to open its eyes and get streetwise to what is happening.

Why is it that all the major global reports saying there is a drastic environmental problem have been fronted and funded by the people who are dismantling the world's ecology? The Club of Rome was set up by these people and it became the engine room of the environmental movement through the 70s which exploded in the 80s.

The Trilateral Commission, of all people, produced a book in the run-up to the 1992 Earth

Summit in Brazil, saying: "environmental problem, something must be done." Why? Because of true concern about pollution? I don't believe it. Look at the list of corporate polluters who are members of the Trilateral Commission.

No, if you want global control and global law, you have to have global problems which can justify global solutions. As a result of some of the treaties like the Bio-Diversity Treaty, great chunks of land are being handed over to the United Nations, exactly as planned. This gathers more global control in fewer hands. I detail the manipulation of the environmental movement in my book "... and the truth shall set you free."

There is nothing more manipulable than genuineness that is not streetwise. That applies to the environmental movement, the New Age, and the UFO movement.

What Future Do You Want?

Jon Rappoport (JR): What do you see as a possible portrait, of say, 50 years down the line here? The human future. Do you think there's a chance that enough people will wake up to this kind of discussion we are having here so they begin, truthfully, to create their own realities? And if they were to do that, what would the landscape actually look like? How would the world be essentially different from what it is today?

David Icke (DI): Exactly how it would look would depend on the decisions that people made. Certainly it would be very, very different from today. The manipulation of the consensus is part of the control. You manipulate for a consensus you want to happen. This idea that to have harmony and peace in the world you have to have consensus is not true. Diversity is freedom. You can have diversity and harmony. You can have disagreement and harmony if people are respecting each other's right to their view and their life, so long as they don't impose it on other people.

What I do see, and I've spoken in, goodness knows, it must be twelve countries this year, I do see a global awakening going on. It is not the majority yet. Some of it is extremely ungrounded but people are waking up and asking questions and no longer buying the reality they're being asked to live and accept.

I do think we are now in the healing crisis of the human race and the healing crisis of the Earth. We are very much in a transition period between the world as it's been and the world as it is going to be. I think the next few years are going to be very bumpy as the old starts to crumble and yet does not want to go, and the other new reality starts to emerge.

I do think it is going to be quite a chaotic period, because I think chaos is going to be manipulated to create a situation in which the elite can offer solutions to the chaos — namely a very centralized world. We have the opportunity now — I think there is a Chinese word for crisis which means both danger and opportunity — we have the opportunity now as the old starts to crumble where we can accept the "new" world created by the same people who controlled the old, or we can take this opportunity to go in another direction. The first thing we need to do is to set ourselves free by stepping out from the prisons of control and imposition.

If we do those things, this whole edifice of control, which is based on holding consciousness in a very narrow sheep pen of reality, crumbles. I think out of that will come a world in which the structures of today will not be there anymore. We will go from the pyramid to the circle, in which everyone's contribution will be respected, whatever it may be. A beautiful piece of art will be respected in the same way that someone's sweeping the streets will be respected. We won't judge each other on the basis of the system's values, when really we are on an eternal journey of evolution through experience. All experience.

Someone who is sweeping the streets, oh, he's just a roadsweeper, what a failure, is today's response. But, if he actually learns from the experiences his life gives him, at the end of his life he is going to be far more successful than a guy who's made vast amounts of units of exchange on a computer screen in Wall Street, but has not learned from experience. The real "winner" at the end of this physical experience will be the roadsweeper.

I think that our values, in the way we judge each other, therefore pressure each other, are simply the system's values. Everyone wants to feel successful and have confirmation that we're okay people. We want others to say, hey, he's successful, she's successful. You feel good when people say that.

To be successful in a way that attracts that confirmation you have to be successful by the definitions of success that most people use, i.e. lots of money, big house, good job. The vast majority of people are living lives and doing jobs they really don't want to do.

If we think the acquisition of money is the only form of success, a big house, a big car and all this stuff, then we are usually going to have to play the system's game to get that and therefore we are completely under its control. We need to look at each other and our definition of "success" in a very different way.

Another Brick in the Wall

Jon Rappoport (JR):   I've read some interesting accounts of schools that departed from the norm and tried to set up something like what you are suggesting. Clearly, this is one of the steps that would have to be taken so education would turn into a situation where people would feel encouraged to decide on their own, what is it that I want to do? What gives me the greatest satisfaction?

David Icke (DI): What are your unique gifts?

JR: Yes. What is your choice? What are you being pressured to do? What do you really want to do? If these things became part of our society in some way at the level of education, then I think we could really start to look to some of these changes.

DI: Sure. I think one of the most moving films that I have ever seen is The Dead Poets' Society, which kind of summed up a lot of this stuff. But, of course, the system is there to create clones, not to create thinking, unique people. This is the heart of the indoctrination. Get the child early and you'll control the adult for life.

Education has to change. This is the responsibility of people who choose education as a career.

It is the responsibility of professors and lecturers and teachers to stop playing the system's game and to start saying to children and to students, hey, I am giving you a version of reality here. You don't have to accept it. Think about it, does it make sense? Do you really have to do the jobs that you think you have to? Do you really want to be a banker? What do you really want to do with your life? What's your gift? What's your inspiration?

What I find, and I think this is highly significant, around the world I see the funding of education for art, for music being reduced. There is very good reason for this, I think. As even conventional science accepts, there are two areas of the brain. There's the left brain, which is basically the physical world's version of reality, the so-called "rational," The right brain is the inspirational, which is our connection to a higher level of consciousness. What they want to do is to imprison us in the left brain, into the rational, the physical world reality. The whole "education" system is designed for this. It is left-brain dominated.

Art and music stimulate the right brain. They are the inspirational, creative forces at work and they open up the right brain. When the right brain is stimulated you start to transform your vision of reality. This is why some of the most open-minded people are worse in art and music. Not all of them, but a great ratio of them. It's because the right brain is being stimulated.

Journey of Discovery

Jon Rappoport (JR): I would like to get some sense of the layers that you passed through personally to get to this place that you have been describing, this point of view. I understand that you worked for the BBC in England. You were obviously witness to a great many stories passing through. I would like to hear about where you came from originally.

David Icke (DI): It's a long story. There are many, many elements to it, all of which are vital to where I am now. I was born in Leicester in England and I was from what they call a "working-class" background. One of my earliest memories was every Thursday afternoon going around the back of the factory where my father worked so he could hand over the pay packet he had just been given for that week. This was so my mother could pay for that night's dinner. We were really hand-to-mouth. But it was a great experience. It allows you to appreciate things that come to you later in life.

I was a kid who always had this feeling that I was here to do something, but I had no idea what it was. Early in my life I had a fear of dying. The reason was that I did not want to die before I had done whatever I had come to do. I was a kid who really lacked confidence in myself, but then I realized I was good at soccer and my self-esteem increased.

These emotional prisons I'm exposing today — I've experienced all of them. I am not claiming to be holier than thou or walking on water. I know what it's like. It has been important to the work that I am doing that I have experienced them. If you are trying to make a connection with somebody, actually understanding how they are feeling, or what they are going through, it's absolutely vital to have experienced what they are experiencing. This is why the best people to help alcoholics are former alcoholics. The best people to help drug addicts are people who have been addicted to drugs and come through it. They understand. There is no such thing as a wasted experience.

I became a soccer player and eventually, through a series of tremendous bits of "luck," I turned professional. I was a goalkeeper. I played until I was 21 when serious arthritis ended my career. It is now dramatically improved since I changed attitudes in the last ten years.

I was 21 and my football career was over. It was all that I have ever wanted to do in my life. The arthritis started when I was 15-1/2, only six months after I had left school to join the soccer club, Coventry City. The latter part of my career, the last two years, I played in absolute agony from the arthritis.

This activated something within me to overcome challenges, emotional challenges and physical challenges. Also, my father, when I was a kid, was challenging me emotionally right through my childhood in various ways. I could not do anything right, and all this stuff. It was an emotional onslaught.

We attract to us experiences that we need, not necessarily what we want. Although I could have throttled my father when I was 15, I later realized what he had given me and what I had given myself by making the choice before incarnation to be with him. He had activated my emotional steel and my mental steel to overcome his onslaught. So when the stuff starting hitting the fan in the early 1990s, I was able to come through it. I'll come to that in a minute.

At 21, I could not walk, I had no job, my soccer club (now Hereford United) canceled my contract because I could not play anymore. I had £36 in the world, no job, no income, and a mortgage of £66 a month. This was 1973 and life was fun!

I decided I wanted to be a presenter for the biggest BBC sports program, Grandstand. People thought it was funny, impossible. You know, these things happen to other people. Because most people in the world think these things happen to other people, they do. I've never thought that. I got a job on a local newspaper. If its circulation had been human it would have been on a life support machine. But it got me in there.

I progressed pretty quickly into daily newspapers, radio, then television. I was a news journalist, and I worked for BBC Television News. In the

80s I was offered a job by BBC Sports, and I became a front man for sports programs, among them Grandstand. I'd "made it." Once I had reached that goal, though, it was like, okay, done that, now what next?

I remained in network television as a presenter right through the 1980s, but I started to look at the world in a wider sense, especially the environment and human injustice, or what I thought was injustice.

I eventually became a national spokesman for the British Green Party. What tends to happen in my life is that I decide I want to do something and then it happens very quickly. When I look back I see different, apparently unconnected experiences leading me by the hand to where I am now and giving me what I need to know.

I started a branch of the Green Party on a small island off England's South Coast called the Isle of Wight. Two weeks later I got a letter from the little regional Green Party group in Southern England. The letter said there was a regional meeting in Winchester, in Hampshire, and would we send a representative of our new Party. So I turn up in Winchester.

We are sitting around this big circle, and as usual in Green Party meetings everyone is contemplating their navel, coming to no particular conclusion. They come to the end of this meeting and I am thinking, what a waste of space this has been.

Then one guy says: "I can't be regional representative on National Party Council anymore, I've got to step down." So the chairlady said, "Right, we need another representative of the Regional Party on the National Party Council. Anyone want to put their name forward?" No one responds.

So I am sitting there and I think, well someone better do it. I'll do it. So they have a vote and two people voted against me even though I was the only candidate!

Anyway, another two or three weeks pass. I have now been in the Green Party for about five or six weeks. I turn up at the National Party meeting as the Regional Representative. Just before lunch someone says: "We need Party spokespeople for this year to talk in the media about the Party's policies." They decide to select them after lunch.

I am standing there with my vegetarian lunch and this guy comes up to me and says, "You are on the television, aren't you?" I say, "Yeah, that's right."

He says, "You'll be confident speaking in front of the cameras, won't you? Would you want to be a national spokesman? I'll nominate you." So I became a national spokesman for the Green Party. I had been in the Party about five weeks by this time!

When I went to my first press conference it was attended by one journalist and basically a man and a dog. But something was stirring and over the months that followed support for Green Parties and environmental awareness started to increase in Europe.

By the spring of 1989 I had been a national spokesman for about a year. There was a European election and the Greens got 15% of the popular vote, two million votes I think it was. This was extraordinary because we had never been much above 1% before.

So suddenly I am on the news and being interviewed on current affairs programs. I am a politician now. But I don't feel comfortable doing it. Nevertheless, I saw politics from the inside and that was important. I did not like what I saw, to say the least. Organized (often disorganized) hypocrisy it was. If people saw what goes on, they'd never vote again.

We had a Party Conference, the first one after the big election result. There were cameras everywhere. But the Green Party managed to destroy the opportunity by arguing among themselves. Life went on and the popularity of the Green Party started to wane rapidly. Understandably so. It was just a blip. If Greens had got into power, they would not have known what to do. Talk about disorganized.

I wrote a book called It Doesn't Have to Be Like This, which looked at the environmental and human state of the world. I wanted to write a book that set out the agenda of the Green movement and its spiritual, political, and economic philosophy in words that people could understand. In the writing of it and the researching of it, I came to the conclusion that unless there was some unknown force that I had never considered before, which could intervene into this mess we had created, we as a planet were in serious, serious trouble.

I had always rejected religion and I still do, and I had also rejected the establishment-science idea that we are all a cosmic accident and we come from oblivion and we are heading for oblivion. But I never really thought about the alternative to this.

I was working for the Green Party and the BBC and traveling around, and as 1990 began some strange things started to happen to me. On the speaking tour for It Doesn't Have to Be Like This, I found myself in Nottingham with a Green Party member in his house. He started talking to me about other dimensions, spirits and stuff like that. He gets up in the middle of this conversation and walks over to his bookshelf and says he is being asked to give me a book. He hands it to me. I looked at him. I said, "What do you mean you're being told to give me this? There's only me and you in the room. What are you talking about? Who's telling you?"

He said, "My spirit guide." I thought, oh my God, is that the time? I must be going. What's all this about?

But I read the book he gave me. It was about the life of a psychic. Some of it felt okay, about other dimensions and spirits. Then as these weeks passed I started to sense a sort of presence around me. I remember I got so fed up with it. I was in a hotel room while I was working for the BBC, it was the Kensington Hilton in London. I remember sitting in this hotel room and I just said to no one in particular, "Look, if you are there, will you please contact me, because you are driving me up the wall."

A few days later I am at Ryde, the town on the Isle of Wight where I lived at the time, and I am playing soccer with my son, Gareth, down at the seafront. I had just bought a book called The End of Nature, which I still have not read, because of what happened. I said to Gareth, we're going to have some lunch, and we went down to this little cafe at the railway station which is on the seafront at Ryde. When we got there it was full of people, so I said we'll walk up into the town and find somewhere else. At which point one of the railwaymen at the station started talking to me about soccer. After this conversation had ended I realized Gareth was missing. I couldn't see him. I knew he was interested in steam trains and the newpaper shop at the station had a lot of steam train books, so I thought that's where he is. I walked in and there he was reading a steam train book. I said to him, "Gareth, let's go, we're going to have our lunch."

I turned to go and I'm not kidding you, it was like two magnets were pulling my feet down. Something in my head said very strongly, it was a very strong feeling, not a voice, a feeling — "go and look at the books at the far side." That was where they displayed what we call in Britain, Mills and Boon books about tall, dark, handsome soldiers meeting perfect English Roses and living happily ever after. I thought, why should I go over there? I already have a book, I just paid £13 for it, The End of Nature. What do I want another book for?

But the feeling was so strong that I walk over and I see this book in among the Mills and Boons. It was called Mind to Mind. So I turn it over and I see the word "psychic" and I think, my God, not another. I'd started to bump into psychics a lot. I read that this lady was a healer, a hands-on healer and a psychic.

I read the book and I wrote to her. She rings me back within days and I go over to see her. The first two times I went she did hands-on healing and I felt good. There was certainly something going on. We chatted about things that had happened to me.

The third time I went — I only went four times — the third time she's got her hands on my leg doing this healing. I'm on this couch. What I felt was like a spider's web going onto my face. She said in her book that psychic energy can feel like a spider's web on your face. I thought, what's going on? It was all new to me, this stuff. Just as that happened, she jumps back in her chair and she says, "My goodness, I'll have to close my eyes for this one." I am thinking, oh my God, what's happening? She starts giving me information. She saw this figure and she kept giving me this stuff. She said, "I'm being asked to tell you this." This is March, 1990.

One message said:

"You have not come here to be healed, but one day you will be completely healed. You have come here to be contacted. We know you wanted us to contact you but the time wasn't right."

I was told there were going to be great changes in the world, a big consciousness shift, that a great shadow was going to be lifted from the Earth. I was going to write five books in three years about this subject, the message said. It sounded like nonsense. After all, getting five books published in three years is hard enough, let alone writing them on a subject I knew nothing about. But you know, I did it to the month. I did not even realize I had done it until I checked back. I thought, shit, three years exactly, the fifth book. And I've always had this feeling that I had a job to do, that I was here for a specific reason.

The messages also said I was eventually going to be talking on a global scale about these subjects. It sounded so strange. I was a television presenter, I was introducing the soccer and I'm told I'm going to do all this. I was told that I would get out of politics because politics was non-spiritual. One message said that the spiritual road was tough and no one made it easy. That's probably the most accurate flippin' thing I've ever been told in my life, given what was to happen!

I started writing a book called Truth Vibrations* about my experiences and what was happening to me. Then I got sacked by the BBC, so my job was finished. I stopped being a spokesman for the British Green Party, so my politics was finished. I got sacked from the BBC for my political work. They denied it but that is exactly what they did it for. I got letters galore of commendation for my work for the BBC. I had contract after contract renewed. As soon as I got involved in politics and I started to get high profile, bang, gone.

----

* Second edition (Gateway Books, 1994).

But, of course, from the big-picture point of view, it was exactly as planned. It was time for me to move on. For 3 years after that I earned virtually nothing. My bank account was like a financial road traffic accident. It was only the money that I had earned in television that allowed me to get through those years.

I finished this book, Truth Vibrations. Much of it was written in a fog, which is, I think, why so many people have resonated with it. I was trying to work out what was happening to me. We are all in a fog when we first wake up. The book went to the printers in very late 1990 and I got this overwhelming feeling I had to go to Peru. Why, I don't know. I just felt, go to Peru. I had never been there, never thought about it before.

I then bump unto this psychic, another psychic. She says to me, "Have you ever thought about going to Peru?" So I went to Peru on nothing more than my intuition. I end up at Lima Airport about six o'clock in the morning. Lima Airport is one of the hell-holes of the world. Peru is beautiful. Lima Airport — if the planet was a human being they would put the enema in Lima Airport.

I got my bag and I stood there in this airport lounge in the early hours of the morning. There are just loads and loads of people. This guy comes forward and asks me where I'm going. I didn't know. I just blurted out, "Cuzco," which is the only place I had read about. It was the center of the Inca civilization in the ancient world and probably inspired by Atlantean knowledge.

He said, have you got a hotel? I said no. Have you got a ticket? No. So he said, I'll get you a ticket, I'll get you a hotel. I followed him through the crowd like a little boy lost. He gets me a ticket and a hotel. Then I go across to the Cuzco check-in for a flight that is leaving very shortly and there is a massive queue. I go to the back because I'm English, you know. The English love queuing! He said, no, no. He ushers me down to the front of the queue where his mate is doing the checking in. I'm on the plane to Cuzco.

When I get there I meet a Peruvian guide who takes people to the sacred sites. When I went round to meet him the first morning, he was asleep on the floor and the first words he said to me were, "Did you have any dreams last night?" I thought, that's a funny opening line. But I'd had a very vivid dream that one of my two middle front teeth had fallen out. He said, "Is your father or grandfather still alive?" I said my father is, yeah. He says, "That dream is usually symbolic of your father or your grandfather dying." I thought, this guy's going to be a bunch of laughs. But when I eventually made a phone call out of Peru a few days later — which is not easy once you are outside Lima — my wife told me that my father had died. Actually the funeral had already taken place by the time I made contact.

I went to many sacred sites in Peru, like Machu Picchu. The guide booked us into a hotel in a place called Puno which is not far from Lake Titicaca in Southern Peru. The hotel was called the Sillustani. On the walls were pictures of an Inca "burial" site after which the hotel was named.

Any time archeologists find a pile of stones they always call it a burial site. I think the ancients must have spent their whole lives burying each other! It's never an energy site or a meditation chamber or anything like that, it's always a burial site. Anyway I say I want to go there and it was out of season so I had to hire a tourist van and driver.

We go off to this place called Sillustani which is about an hour's drive from Puno. It's a beautiful place. It's a big mound or hill with all this stone work on top of it, and then around it is a lagoon. Beautiful. Uninhabited. No houses, nothing, just open land. Beautiful. It was a piercingly hot Peruvian day.

Then we get into the van to go home. About three minutes down the road I am looking out the side of the van window, just daydreaming and I see this mound to my right. I don't normally hear voices, but this time I did hear one or two which were very clear. I was looking at this mound. Basically what I was hearing was, "Come to me, come to me, come to me, over here." So I thought, hell, that mound's talking to me, this is crazy. I said to the driver, "Could you just stop the van, I want to go up that mound." I get out and say I'll be a few minutes. I was actually an hour and a half.

When I get to the top, there is a circle of stones about waist high which obviously has been there a very long time. I stand in the middle of this stone circle, just looking back at where I've come from, Sillustani just across the way, and to the mountains in the distance.

Suddenly I get a repeat, only far stronger, of what happened in the news agent's shop at the train station. I get like two giant electromagnets pulling my feet down to the earth. The bottom of my feet start to burn. Then my arms go in the air. If you hold your arms up for two or three minutes it really starts to ache. Mine stayed like that for, I worked it out later, it must have been over an hour and I didn't feel a thing until it was over and then it was agony. Time was meaningless while all this was happening.

I then heard the clearest voice in my head I have ever heard before or since. It said, "It will be over when you feel the rain." This is not a line you'd invent on a piercing hot Peruvian day when there is not a cloud in the sky. So I am standing there thinking, this is absolutely ludicrous. When I get back to England I am going to get myself a proper job again.

I felt like a drill in the top of my head as well. My hands were burning. I could feel energy pouring out of them like a fireburst. My feet are on fire and my body is shaking like I am plugged into a socket. I kept going in and out of consciousness, like you do when you drive a car and you don't know where the last two miles have gone.

After a while I started to see over the distant mountains a light gray mist and then a dark gray mist. Eventually it was obvious it was raining. So I think, I hope it's coming my way. It is right in the distance at this time. Over the best part of an hour or so, this storm comes towards me and the sun is covered by clouds, the sky is covered by clouds. It starts to thunder and lightning like Hammer House of Horror. I was seeing faces. I couldn't work them out but I was seeing faces in the clouds. Then amid the thunder it started to rain on me.

When the rain hits me it's like someone has flicked off a switch. The energy stops. I stagger forward and my legs are like jelly. My arms are agony around the shoulder muscles and my feet are on fire. The Peruvian guide has got fed up with waiting and he's come up to see what's going on. He's looking at me very strangely. I don't know how long he's been there, but he's looking at me very strangely. "Mad Englishmen," his face seemed to say!

Life wasn't the same after that. Things really started to motor, and changes began to happen very quickly. I went back to England and the book came out. It was met with massive ridicule in Britain. I was talking about everyone being a son of God and everyone being an aspect of the whole.

The press said: "Icke Thinks He's Jesus." "Icke Says He's the Son of God Who's Come to Save the World." I was on the front page of all the tabloids. There was massive ridicule. But it gave me a colossal emotional experience which transformed me into a very different person.

Anyway, I couldn't be the reincarnation of Jesus because I come from a place called Leicester and there's no way you'd find three wise men and a virgin there! Sorry Leicester, just a joke.

The Ridicule Years

David Icke (DI): The reaction was amazing. For two years I could not walk down any street in Britain without being laughed at by large numbers of people. Going into a bar was a waste of time. It was a nightmare. At this time I began talking around the universities. It was like walking into the lions' den. I remember speaking to a thousand people at one university. The hall was sold out because people came to laugh. It was going to be lots of fun. When I walked on the stage it was fifteen minutes before I could start because of the noise and plastic cups being thrown at me.

I said to them: You think I am mentally ill then, do you? "Yeah, yeah, yeah" came the mass reply.

So, I said, what does it say about you then? You have paid to come and ridicule someone you believe is mentally ill. What does that say about you?

Silence.

They had realized what we all need to realize, that whenever we speak or act, we are making a statement about ourselves and no one else.

In those days, I was going through a very rapid transformation from what I had been, to what I was becoming. That initial transformation was like a dam bursting. Suddenly my mind was filled with perceptions, concepts, information that flooded into my consciousness. It was like sitting in a room with 50 television sets on, all tuned to different stations, trying to make sense of all of them. This only lasted about three months but it was a real, real challenge.

We draw to us what we need and that whole nightmare experience gave me two essential gifts: First it allowed me to step out of the prison that most people live in, the fear of what others think of them. Most people are not doing what they want to do, saying what they want to say, being what they want to be, because they fear what other people think of them. And because of that they conform to what other people think is right, to avoid being ridiculed and condemned for the crime of being different. This is the key prison that allows the Brotherhood to control people. I stepped out of that as a result of all this ridicule and I was freer than I had ever been.

Those people who ridiculed me actually helped set me free. The other thing was that I was being ridiculed overwhelmingly for what I was not saying and not standing for. The newspapers were simply lying about me on many occasions, and people believed them. As a result I could see very clearly how easy it was to condition and manipulate the thinking of vast numbers of people by pounding out a theme through the mainstream media. I was living it.

Even today if you say to most people in England my name they will say yeah, he thinks he's Jesus and all that. Discovered religion. That's the funny one, when I am actually challenging the whole basis of religion. The difference between people who have heard me or read my books in England and the people who get their opinions from the papers is simply enormous.

Anyway, it was a great experience for me. I started going around the country talking about the spiritual awakening I was having and how we need to challenge the conditioned belief systems. I started looking at the history of religion and showing how Christianity was just the pagan religions under another name.

The Christian religion as we know it was actually created in 325 A.D. by a Roman Emperor, one Constantine the Great, a Brotherhood creation, who worshipped the sun under the name "Sol Invictus" or "Unconquered Sun." In The Biggest Secret, I will show that Jesus was the latest in a long, long, line of "Sons of God who died so our sins could be forgiven." All the others were pagan sun gods.

From about 1993 onwards I started coming across information of names, dates, places, that showed me increasingly that a few people were running the world. I thought, what's going on here? I've been through this spiritual awakening/nightmare? Now I am getting information about how the world's run by a few people. Then I realized that the two are fundamentally connected. A few control the world by suppressing the spirituality and the uniqueness of the mass of the people. They detach them from their higher self.

It is very simple. One of the states of being it is easiest to manipulate is self-righteousness. So much of religion is self-righteousness at war with itself, creating divide-and-rule, causing conflict between people. All you have to do basically is set the norms of society and you run the world, in effect, because the mass of the people will conform to those norms either because they don't think for themselves or they are frightened to be different. Sheep are just the same.

The Human Herd

David Icke (**DI**): Sheep are controlled by the "baa baa" mentality, most of them following the one in front. The rest are rounded up by fear of the sheep dog. Whole herds of sheep, flocks of sheep are controlled in that way all over the world every day. The human race is the two-legged version. We actually out-sheep the sheep. We follow the ones in front because they have letters after their name, or they are a prime minister or they're a doctor, a scientist, a businessman, or a bank manager. Or even the guy down the street who has a friend who knows a friend who said so and so. We just follow the herd without thinking or questioning where the one out in front is leading us. That's why the Brotherhood have been in control for so long.

Jon Rappoport (**JR**): What about the people who have realized that what we are being asked to conform to is fundamentally ridiculous?

DI: The overwhelming majority of them still conform to these norms because they are terrified of being different and saying things that are different and living in a different way. They fear what other people think of them. They fear the reaction of others. The human sheep don't need the sheepdog because we police each other.

Most people who are conforming to norms while not believing in them keep their mouths shut and their heads down. This is not because they fear what the people in power will think about them being different. It's because they fear what their mothers will say about them, or the guys at work, or the people down at the bar. In other words, what's terrifying people into conforming to these norms is the anticipated reaction of all the other people who are conforming to the norms. We are policing each other. We conform to the prison and then act as a prison warder to everyone else.

This means that whoever sets the "norms," creates the limits of this mental and emotional sheep pen, which imprisons people in a desperately narrow area of their consciousness.

Building the Sheep Pen

David Icke (DI): If you can set the norms you run the world. How do you do this? By controlling the mantra messages that come through the education system and the media. Education seems to be a wonderful thing. I agree, so it's about time we had some. We do not have education today, we have indoctrination.

The teachers become teachers by telling the system what it wants to hear because that is the only way they pass their exams. If they don't absorb the system's version of life, they don't become teachers and lecturers. Then they must tell this same story to the students of the next generation. Otherwise they won't stay professors and teachers. Their students write all this stuff down, and if they don't tell their exam paper what the system wants to hear they don't pass their exams. It is a self-perpetuating cycle.

The education system, or what passes for it, is the indoctrination of each generation. The media pounds out the same version of reality day after day after day, because journalists are perpetuating the conditioning they have also taken on. What do the media take as their reference point for how they judge people and events? They use the "norms" in society. So if you set the norms you not only create the sheep pen for the human race, you set the reference point for how the mainstream media record the world. Therefore everyone operating outside the norms of the public arena is ridiculed and condemned by the media. Once you have conditioned one generation to your narrow version of reality, they will, as parents and teachers, indoctrinate the next generation to believe the same thing. So it gets passed on across the generations.

People give away their uniqueness and their right to think to someone else. If you look throughout human history the same themes are there. The Brotherhood in its various forms and expressions has put on a pedestal various figures like Jesus, Mohammed, and Krishna. They are Brotherhood creations and they have held them up as perfect. They have said we are not perfect, we're just ordinary and powerless. It means that if you can condition people to believe that they are ordinary and powerless and insignificant then they will live ordinary, powerless and insignificant lives. You can run the show without challenge.

A Time to Awaken

David Icke (DI): The great news is that more and more people are waking up. The transformation is happening. But if it is going to be effective, people need to live their own truths, express and celebrate their own uniqueness, and not conform to someone else's version of reality. Once we live our own truth, there will be endless unique realities and the Brotherhood will no longer be able to control from the center by manipulating "norms."

The transformation and the bringing down of this edifice of power and manipulation doesn't require guns, smoke-filled rooms, or new political movements. It requires each of us to come into our own unique power and to celebrate our unique truth. This will release incredible amounts of suppressed creativity which at the moment is manifesting itself in very negative ways.

The creative force is enormously powerful and needs to be expressed in some form. When you allow it to flow, it manifests in a balanced way in creativity of a positive kind. When you suppress it, the creative force can be very destructive. I believe this force, when suppressed, manifests itself as crime and violence. Then the system says the only way to stop this is with more suppression, more laws, more powers for enforcement agencies, more guns, bigger prisons and sentences. You further suppress the creative energy and you get more and more violence and the vicious circle becomes a downward spiral.

Most of the creativity that people wish to express would take them outside the hassle-free zone's version of "normality." Therefore they are suppressing their creative energy, because to express it would involve them being different and they are terrified of doing that. Sexual suppression is another block on the flow of the creative force.

For me three things would transform the world and bring an end to the Brotherhood's house of cards. And it is a house of cards. It depends on us being a fraction of who we are, otherwise we could not be manipulated as we are. Those three things are these:

One: Each of us steps out of the fear of what other people think of us and expresses our God-given uniqueness. At that point we cease to be a sheep and we cease to follow the herd.

Two: We allow other people to express their uniqueness, whatever that is, without ridicule and condemnation for the crime of being different. Indeed, we encourage diversity because diversity means, among many other things, that we have far more evolutionary opportunities for learning and experience. We evolve quicker.

When we set others free to express their true self, we cease to be a police force of the herd, we cease to be a sheepdog.

Three: No one imposes their beliefs or desires on anyone else, so always respecting another's right to free will. This is the balance point in which we are constantly aware of how our actions affect others.

Those three things, if we did them, would set the world free. It would demolish the foundation of the Brotherhood. In short, we need to love and respect ourselves and love and respect each other. To set ourselves free and set others free. You can't have one without the other. Love is, has always been, and will always be, the answer. Love is freedom, freedom is love.

As I travel around the world talking in many different countries, I see two things happening. People are awakening spiritually to other versions of life, and the veil is lifting on this manipulation. There is a vibrational magnetic change going on around the planet. It is affecting people's emotions, thinking, physical bodies, everything. This is the time of an enormous evolutionary leap for those who wish to grasp it.

When you start the spiritual journey you attract to you experiences which bring to the surface all that you have wished to suppress, so you can cleanse that level of self, remove that vibrational prison and reconnect with who you really are. The same is happening collectively. All that we have wished to go into denial about, collectively, what we have not wished to talk about, is coming to the surface where we have to face it and heal it. That is why, at the same time these spiritual alarm clocks are going off in more and more people, the three-dimensional evidence of the Brotherhood is coming to center stage as never before.

This is the time of the apocalypse. By that I do not mean the end of the world. The real meaning of apocalypse, as I understand it, is the "revealing," the "unveiling." That is the time we are living in. We are in the healing crisis of the human race and the healing crisis of the Earth. The cause of the disease is rising to the surface so we can face it and heal it. Some in the New Age movement run away from information about the global manipulation because they say it is "negative." They are missing the point, I feel. Truth is never negative, whatever the truth is. Avoiding or perverting the truth is negative. The hidden cancer in the heart of humanity is now increasingly no longer hidden. Therefore we can remove it and step into the light of multi-dimensional freedom.

It's a great time to be alive because we are living the change, not just sitting around hoping for it. We chose to be here at this moment. We gave ourselves the gift of playing a part in the amazing transformation that awaits us.

Okay, what are we waiting for?

Let's get on with it!

Lightning Source UK Ltd.
Milton Keynes UK
UKOW051819270612

195135UK00001B/45/A